JEWISH
FAITH *in* AMERICA

SHELLEY M. BUXBAUM AND
SARA E. KARESH

J. **GORDON MELTON**, SERIES EDITOR

Facts On File, Inc.

JEWISH FAITH IN AMERICA
Faith in America

Facts On File, Inc.
132 West 31st Street
New York NY 10001

Library of Congress Cataloging-in-Publication Data

Buxbaum, Shelley M.
    Jewish faith in America / Shelley M. Buxbaum, Sara E. Karesh.
        p.cm. — (Faith in America)
    Includes bibliographical references and index.
    ISBN: 0-8160-4986-6
        1. Judaism—United States—History 2. Jews—United States—History 3. United States—Ethnic relations.   I. Karesh, Sara E. II. Title. III. Series.

    BM205 .B89 2002
    296'0973—dc21   2002029392

Facts On File books are available at special discounts when purchased in bulk quantities for businesses, associations, institutions, or sales promotions. Please call our Special Sales Department in New York at (212) 967-8800 or (800) 322-8755.

You can find Facts On File on the World Wide Web at http://www.factsonfile.com

Produced by the Shoreline Publishing Group LLC
Editorial director: James Buckley Jr.
Editor: Beth Adelman
Designed by Thomas Carling, Carling Design, Inc.
Photo research: Laurie Schuh

Photo credits:
Cover: AP/Wide World (3); Photodisc, bottom center. American Jewish Archives: 26, 30, 33, 41, 44, 77, 82, 92, 104, 116; American Jewish Historical Society: 34; AP/Wide World: 36, 51, 57, 69, 70, 88, 96, 109; The Art Archive/Museo Tridentino Arte Sacra Trento/Dagli Orti (A): 6; Corbis: 72, 98, 100; Digital Stock: 14, 17; Jewish Community Center: 87; Bob Luckey/Greenwich Time: 112; Courtesy NASA: 111; Stock Montage: 9, 20; Urban Archives/Temple University: 52.

Printed in the United States of America

VB 10 9 8 7 6 5 4 3 2 1

This book is printed on acid-free paper.

CONTENTS

FOREWORD

AMERICA BEGINS A NEW MILLENNIUM AS ONE OF THE MOST RELIGIOUSLY diverse nations of all time. Nowhere else in the world do so many people—offered a choice free from government influence—identify with such a wide range of religious and spiritual communities. Nowhere else has the human search for meaning been so varied. In America today, there are communities and centers for worship representing all of the world's religions.

The American landscape is dotted with churches, temples, synagogues, and mosques. Zen Buddhist zendos sit next to Pentecostal tabernacles. Hasidic Jews walk the streets with Hindu swamis. Most amazing of all, relatively little conflict has occurred among religions in America. This fact, combined with a high level of tolerance of one another's beliefs and practices, has let America produce people of goodwill ready to try to resolve any tensions that might emerge.

The Faith in America series celebrates America's diverse religious heritage. People of faith and ideals who longed for a better world have created a unique society where freedom of religious expression is a keynote of culture. The freedom that America offers to people of faith means that not only have ancient religions found a home here, but that newer ways of expressing spirituality have also taken root. From huge churches in large cities to small spiritual communities in towns and villages, faith in America has never been stronger. The paths that different religions have taken through American history is just one of the stories readers will find in this series.

Like anything people create, religion is far from perfect. However, its contribution to the culture and its ability to help people are impressive, and these accomplishments will be found in all the books in the series. Meanwhile, awareness and tolerance of the different paths our neighbors take to the spiritual life has become an increasingly important part of citizenship in America.

Today, more than ever, America as a whole puts its faith in freedom—the freedom to believe.

Jewish Faith in America

While America is often thought of as a Christian country, Judaism has been a part of it from the beginning—at least from the arrival of the first Europeans. Jews could be found among the parties of different European explorers and in 1654, the first Jewish community was established in the then Dutch settlement of New Amsterdam (now New York). The Jewish community grew slowly through the colonial period, then expanded dramatically through the immigration of Jews from Europe, especially during the early 20th century.

American Jews quickly integrated into the economic life of the American colonies, and have been an important part of almost every aspect of life in the United States in the years since the American Revolution. They have been especially outstanding as doctors, lawyers, psychologists, and entertainers, and increasingly contribute to every area of public service. Their success has been especially noteworthy in the face of the waves of discrimination they have often had to endure.

America has become the home to a culturally rich Jewish religious community, one that now enjoys a new level of diversity that has become integral to Jewish existence in the 21st century. In America, unique forms of Jewish religious life—first Reform Judaism and then Conservative and Reconstructionist Judaism—were allowed to emerge and flourish. Here they found room to mature, and from America they were exported to Jewish communities worldwide.

Jewish Faith in America opens the door on America's Jewish community, offers insights into its religious beliefs and practices, including its significant relationship to the modern nation of Israel, and explains its unique way among the many paths of spirituality. Judaism is an ancient religion that has truly become a modern American faith.

— *J. Gordon Melton, Series Editor*

INTRODUCTION
by Rabbi Mitchell M. Hurvitz

Jewish Origins And Beliefs

THE HISTORICAL ORIGINS OF THE JEWISH FAITH BEGIN WITH THE ancient Israelites, who lived more than 5,700 years ago. The history of the Israelites is recorded within the Hebrew Bible. Jews call their Bible the Tanakh, a word made up of three Hebrew letters—T,N, and KH. They refer to the three parts of the Bible: the Law (called Torah in Hebrew), the Prophets (Nevi'im), and the Writings (Ketuvim). Since Jews do not embrace the New Testament of Christianity as part of their holy canon, Judaism does not use the term "Old Testament."

While the actual historical facts of the Tanakh often cannot be verified, traditional Judaism asserts that the history of the Israelites, as recorded in the Bible, is, in fact, true.

Regardless of its historical accuracy, through the Bible all Jews share a common story. Israelite history, as recorded in the Tanakh, begins with the patriarchs and matriarchs (fathers and mothers of the religion) described in the book of Genesis: Abraham and his wife Sarah; Isaac and his wife Rebecca; and Jacob and his wives Rachel and Leah. According to the Bible, God spoke to Abraham and told him to leave his home in Harran and go to the land of Canaan. In this land, God promised to make Abraham's descendants a great people.

The Israelite patriarchs and matriarchs settled in the land of Canaan. Jacob, the third and last patriarch, had a dream in which he struggled with God. In this dream, Jacob's name was changed to Israel, which literally means "one who struggled with God." With this new name, the Israelite nation was born.

Jacob had 12 children, one of whom he favored over the others. This child, Joseph, was betrayed by his jealous siblings, and sold into slavery in Egypt. Through life's circumstances, Joseph came to the attention of the pharaoh (the king) of Egypt and, with his leadership abilities, rose to second in power in Egypt. He helped the pharaoh avert a famine in Egypt by foreseeing the catastrophe and shaping plans to store food. When the famine struck all the neighboring countries, the Israelites had to go to Egypt to seek food, and, ultimately, to confront the brother they betrayed.

Joseph reconciled with his siblings and the Israelites settled in the land of Goshen, a fertile piece of Egypt. There the children of Israel grew in number, developing into the 12 tribes of Israel. Exodus, one of the books of the Bible, declares that eventually a new pharaoh arose in Egypt who did not recall the merits performed by Joseph and believed the Israelite presence posed a threat to Egypt. This pharaoh enslaved the Israelites, so that they would serve his whim.

Moses

During 400 years of slavery, the Israelite nation continued to grow. In a few dramatic lines at the beginning of Exodus, we learn that the pharaoh ordered all newborn male babies to be killed because the number of Israelites was growing so rapidly. The story continues with details of a baby who was placed in a basket in the Nile River to avoid death. This child was drawn out of the river by the pharaoh's daughter, who adopted him as her own. She named the baby Moses, which means, "drawn out."

The baby grew up as an Egyptian prince, but the Bible tells us that his nursemaid was, in fact, his own Israelite mother. The assumption is made that through this relationship with his mother, Moses learned of his own Israelite heritage.

As an adult, Moses rejected the immorality of slavery, and, in saving the life of an Israelite slave, he killed an Egyptian taskmaster. Because of his actions, Moses was forced to flee from Egypt to the neigh-

boring nation of Midian. There he made a home with a priest, Jethro, married his daughter, and embraced a quiet shepherd's life. But Moses' tranquility was disturbed when he was called to a mountain, where he had a vision of a burning bush that was not consumed by the fire. Exodus says that at that place, the God of the Israelites spoke to Moses and told him to go to Egypt and, with God's help, free the Israelite people from slavery and return them to their holy land.

Laws and Leaders

Moses fulfilled his mission; the Israelites were freed and brought to Mount Sinai. There they received God's 10 Commandments, which presented a revolutionary code for living. They also received the holy Torah, also known as the Five Books of Moses. These are the first five books of the Bible: Genesis, Exodus, Leviticus, Numbers, and Deuteronomy.

The Torah may be compared to the United States Constitution. It contains a set of laws that are the foundation of the Israelite nation. Like the United States Constitution, the law is both dynamic and somewhat flexible; it is a document that continues to evolve and be interpreted and reinterpreted over the centuries.

When the Israelites resettled in the land of Canaan, they were ruled first by judges. Eventually, they asked God for a king, and were led first by King Saul and then by King David. David established Jerusalem as the capital of the Israelite nation. Under David's leadership, the Israelites reached their pinnacle of power. On David's death, his youngest son, Solomon, inherited the throne. Solomon built a temple in Jerusalem that was the central worshiping place of the Israelites.

When Solomon died, there was a civil division among the Israelites. The 10 tribes of the Northern Kingdom set up a competing central worship area. Ultimately, the Northern Kingdom was conquered by Assyria and these 10 tribes disappeared. The Southern Kingdom remained in place with the other two tribes. The predominant tribe was Judah, which is where the word "Jew" comes from.

In 586 B.C.E. Solomon's Temple was destroyed by the Babylonians. The first exile occurred, and the Israelite political, religious, and economic leaders were forced to live in Babylon. It is during this time

The Books of the Tanakh

LAW (TORAH)	Kings	Nahum	The Song of Songs
Genesis	Isaiah	Habakkuk	Ruth
Exodus	Jeremiah	Zephaniah	Lamentations
Leviticus	Ezekiel	Haggai	Ecclesiastes
Numbers	Hosea	Zechariah	Esther
Deuteronomy	Joel	Malachi	Daniel
PROPHETS (NEVI'IM)	Amos	WRITINGS (KETUVIM)	Ezra
Joshua	Obadiah	Psalms	Nehemiah
Judges	Jonah	Proverbs	Chronicles
Samuel	Micah	Job	

that the Israelite religion began to transform into a religion that more closely resembles the Judaism of today. The Jews began to find ways to worship even though their temple had been destroyed and their political leaders were in exile.

Judaism Expands

After Persia conquered Babylon, the exiled Israelites were allowed to return to Jerusalem and rebuild their temple. But even with the new temple, the Israelite customs and beliefs formed in exile remained intact. Over the centuries the temple of Jerusalem would be conquered and defiled by other nations, and was finally destroyed by the Romans in the year 70 C.E. This destruction resulted in the second exile, called diaspora, which dispersed the Jewish people throughout the world.

There were many sects that claimed they were the ones who continued the true religion of the Israelites, but ultimately the Pharisees won out. The teachers of the Pharisees were called rabbis, and this is the real beginning of the Jewish faith as it is practiced in modern times.

The rabbis retained the Torah as their constitution, but, from the third century through the ninth century C.E., they also wrote down their oral traditions and interpretations of the Law. Ultimately, the legal and ethical teachings of the rabbis was collected into a book called the Talmud, which literally means "the teachings." The rabbis constructed a Jewish legal and ethical system that enabled the Jewish people to have a portable nation—a nation without a capital or a temple. Wherever Jews went to live, their rabbis, who acted as legislators, judges, chief executives, and diplomats to the non-Jewish leaders, guided them.

By then, Jews were spread throughout the world. Both Christian and Muslim lands at times hosted the Jews, sometimes graciously, other times reluctantly. During different periods, some non-Jewish leaders incited violence against the Jews, pursuing forced conversion, murders, and expulsion.

For example, in Spain of 1492, when Christopher Columbus took his famous voyage to the New World, the Spanish king decreed that all the Jews must either convert to Catholicism or leave the country.

Like other religious groups fleeing religious oppression, Jews of the Old World would seek out the New World, which offered promise for a better life.

B.C.E.

These letters stand for the phrase "Before the Common Era," and are used in the same way as historians use the letters B.C.—which stand for "Before Christ"—to refer to events that happened before the year 1 in the common calendar. Events that took place after the birth of Christ are marked with the letters C.E., for "Common Era" (used the same way as A.D.—an abbreviation for the Latin term *Anno Domini*, which means "the Year of Our Lord"). Jewish historians do not accept the divinity of Jesus, and therefore use a term that recognizes the common use of the Christian calendar, but not its religious implications.

God in Judaism

The primary religious belief of Judaism is the belief in one God—a concept known as monotheism. As we will see, there are different models of the Jewish faith, but the belief in the oneness of God is ever-present.

Orthodox Jews pray three times each day: morning, afternoon, and evening. During each of these three daily services, Jews declare the oneness of God. With eyes closed, Jews pronounce the central statement of their religion: "Hear O Israel, the Lord is our God, the Lord is One." According to the rabbis, the eyes are closed because each individual will perceive God in their own unique and personal way.

Here are some of the traditional Jewish teachings about what God is:

- **God is Creator.** God created the universe and all that is in it. God created the intricacies of nature and bestowed the gift of life upon humanity.

- **God is Law-Giver.** God provided humanity with a moral law that teaches right from wrong. With the existence of God, humanity learns that there is an absolute moral voice in the universe.

- **God is History.** God is perceived as interacting in and affecting history, either in a direct or a subtle manner.

- **God is Love.** God teaches that all people are created in the image of God, and are therefore equal and responsible for one another. Humanity is commanded to love and take care of one another and to love their God, who gave them life.

Many Jews embrace a theology of God being omnipotent (all powerful), omniscient (all knowing), and all good. Those who believe this also believe God has created an afterlife, so that while justice may not be found in this world, there is ultimate justice in the eternal life.

Halakhah (Jewish Law)

Because Jews embrace their belief in one God, they attempt to practice God's will. According to the Hebrew Bible, God gave his laws to all of humanity, and made an additional covenant with the Jewish people.

COVENANT

A covenant is a pact that creates obligations for both sides. God promised to give the Jewish people certain benefits, but they also assumed certain obligations.

The first laws given by God to all humanity are referred to as the Seven Laws of Noah. God established these laws in the aftermath of the great flood, with which God intended to destroy the evil that had arisen amidst humanity. The Seven Laws of Noah are understood by the rabbis as God's attempt to recreate and reorder human society. These seven laws are interpreted by the rabbis as commanding numerous responsibilities for all people, but chief among them is the commandment that humanity shall never commit murder. The reason, stated clearly in Genesis, is: "For in His [God's] image, did God make humanity."

When the Israelites received their own set of laws (the 10 Commandments) at Mount Sinai, the Seven Laws of Noah remained intact. There are also many other laws, about how to behave, worship, eat, and even dress, that God gave to the Jewish people through Moses. The reason that God entered into a specific relationship with the Jewish people is so that they would help spread God's teachings in the world.

In reality, this mission has been accomplished. From Judaism has sprung Christianity and Islam. Ultimately, all of Western civilization has received the moral authority of God from the Jewish people. Jesus was a Jew, and the New Testament reflects the Jewish moral code. The Hebrew Bible is included in the Christian Bible. Islam also includes the Hebrew Bible and the New Testament in its holy books, called the Koran. While there are substantial differences in form and practice among the three religions, the primary moral teachings of all three are the same.

Jewish Land and Nationhood

Because the majority of Jewish history has been lived in exile, the Jewish people had to learn to thrive as a nation without any territory. The Jews managed to create a portable law code, but within this construction, the hope was always kept alive that one day the Jewish people might restore their homeland. For 2,000 years this hope remained, and in 1948 the dream was realized with the re-establishment of the Jewish state of Israel, with Jerusalem as its capital.

Since then, many Jews have embraced other adopted homelands or have chosen to remain in the countries of their birth. But the existence of Israel is still important to Jews everywhere. Compare this to a person of Irish descent who is born and raised in America. This person may take great pride in the heritage and accomplishments of Ireland, but America is their home. They may support their ancestral homeland, but they would not imagine loyalty to any other than the country of their birth. So it is with many Jews in America.

American Jews found their country to be the first true non-Jewish society where they could completely be at home. This experience is shared among many peoples of different religions of varied backgrounds. America, having come into existence as a safe haven for the victims of religious persecution, ultimately created a society that protects the religious rights of all, while maintaining a moral code that reflects the Judeo-Christian morality.

American Judaism thrives because the United States encourages freedom of religion. The Constitution protects the minority and encourages the pursuit of one's own particular religious or ethnic background, while cultivating a multi-ethnic, multi-religious loyalty to the common American dream.

Bar mitzvah
Reading from the Torah is a central part of the bar or bat mitzvah. A special pointer, called a yad, is used so that any dirt or oil on the fingertips does not spoil the Torah scrolls.

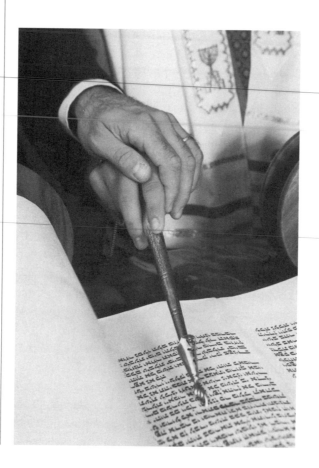

The Jewish Cycle of Life

A Jewish life has its own set of unique milestones. When a baby boy is eight days old, he is circumcised with the appropriate blessing, as Abraham did to his own eight-day-old son Isaac, thousands of years ago. This ceremony is known as *b'rit milah*, which literally means "covenant of circumcision." Today many people call this ceremony a *bris*, which is the European dialect of the Hebrew word *b'rit*.

Since the *b'rit milah* is only for boys entering the Jewish covenant with their God, many modern Jews celebrate a ceremony marking the birth of their daughters. This ceremony is called *simchat bat*, or "the joy of the daughter." While there is no medical aspect to this ceremony, as there is with circumcision, liturgy has been created to mark the significance of one's daughter being born into the Jewish people.

When a boy turns 13 years of age (or 12 for a girl), they become a *bar* (*bat* for a girl) *mitzvah*. The term means "son (or daughter) of the commandment." *Bar/bat mitzvah* means one becomes an adult under Jewish law. In America, a Jewish child celebrates their *bar/bat mitzvah* by learning to lead a congregation in worship, chanting from the sacred scriptures, and teaching an interpretation of Jewish sacred texts. Jewish families celebrate this major transitional rite in the life of their child with a party following the *bar/bat mitzvah* service.

In America, the *bar/bat mitzvah* has become a major family event. It is cause for great jubilation and the opportunity to gather friends and family. The closest approximation to the *bar/bat mitzvah* is a wedding. Since parents don't know when their child will be married, many parents will want to create the opportunity for joyful celebration while they are sure elderly relatives will still be present.

Weddings are joyful gatherings with a specific set of rituals. The ceremony begins with the signing of the *ketubah*, or wedding contract. The *ketubah* is the oldest Jewish legal text used today that is written in Aramaic, which was the language spoken by the Jews 2,000 years ago. Today, the *ketubah* is a symbolic wedding agreement, but no traditional Jewish wedding would begin without the signing of the *ketubah* by two witnesses before the bride and groom stand under the *chuppah*. The *chuppah* is a wedding canopy, which all Jewish couples get married under. The *chuppah* is a symbol of the home the bride and groom will create together.

The Jewish Year

Judaism has a wide variety of holidays and feast days that are celebrated each year at about the same time. The most important Jewish holiday is the weekly celebration of the Sabbath. The 10 Commandments contain only one commandment concerning the observance of a particular ritual. This is the fourth commandment, which declares that Jews must remember and observe their Sabbath.

The Sabbath begins at sunset on Friday and ends at sunset on Saturday night. Jews attend worship services, enjoy festive dinners, study their sacred texts, sing joyous songs, and participate in other meaningful celebrations. For many American families, the Friday night Sabbath dinner is a unique time to gather loved ones, share good food, and enjoy quiet quality time with one another.

10 Days of Awe. The Jewish New Year begins with Rosh HaShanah, literally "head of the year" (usually in September—see page 114 for more about the Jewish calendar and why Jewish holidays do not come on the same day every year). A major custom on Rosh HaShanah is to eat something sweet to show how much a people would like to have a sweet new year. Rosh HaShanah marks the beginning of the 10 Days of Awe, an especially poignant period within the Jewish year that calls for prayerful reflection, repentance for one's sins and the desire to avoid future sinful behavior.

The 10 Days of Awe concludes with Yom Kippur (September or October), the day of atonement. All Jews over the age of *bar/bat mitzvah* are commanded by God to fast from sunset to sunset, unless the fasting makes them ill. It is imagined that God judges each individual on Yom Kippur, deciding whether their life warrants another year in the Book of Life. While this is understood metaphorically by most Jews, they realize their mortality on this day and spend it reflecting on the life they have led and the life they want to lead.

Festival Days. Five days after Yom Kippur is the week-long festival of Sukkot (October). The first of three pilgrimage festivals mentioned in the Bible, Sukkot is also called the Festival of the Booths, because Jewish families build temporary booths where they eat their meals. This is a harvest thanksgiving holiday. Many scholars believe the Pilgrims of Plymouth modeled their own Thanksgiving celebration after the Biblical model of Sukkot.

SPELLING HEBREW

In this book you will find some words, such as Chanukkah and matzah, spelled in a different way than you may be accustomed to seeing. We've chosen spellings that more accurately reflect the way these words are pronounced in Hebrew, which is the language of Judaism.

The Passover seder is a special service and dinner, usually held at home, that retells the story of the Jews' liberation from slavery in Egypt. The special foods eaten at a seder recall different elements of the story.

The final day of Sukkot is followed by a holiday called Simchat Torah (usually in October), which means "the joy of the Torah." We learn from an interpretation of the Biblical text that God was so pleased to have the Israelite people join him for a week-long celebration in Jerusalem, that He prevailed on them to stay on for an extra day or two, thus creating an additional celebration. The Torah is read in a liturgical cycle over the course of a year, and on Simchat Torah the reading of the five books concludes and then the community starts anew.

Purim (February or March) is a holiday commemorating the destruction of an evil man's plan to destroy the Persian Jewish community. Purim celebrates Jewish survival even while remembering the evil that some human beings have attempted to perpetuate against the Jewish people.

Pesach, or Passover (usually in April), is the second of three pilgrimage holidays, and recalls the Israelite liberation from Egypt. This holiday is widely observed among Jews with a Passover seder at home. The word *seder* means "order," and the seder is a special set of rituals

A Popular Holiday In America

Chanukkah, which usually arrives in December, is a minor Jewish holiday. It celebrates the Macabbees' defeat of the Assyrians and the rededication of the Temple in Jerusalem. The holiday had strong nationalistic implications. The rabbis originally were uncomfortable with Chanukkah because they felt it celebrated the works of people and not the works of God. This is why the story of Chanukkah is not included in the Bible. However, the rabbis respected the Jewish people's desire to celebrate independence from an oppressor, and they established a religious ritual to mark God's presence. At Chanukkah, Jews light a menorah—a special candle holder with eight branches. (A ninth candle, called the *shamash*, is used to light all the others.) The menorah recalls a miracle God performed: When the Temple was rededicated, a small amount of holy oil that was only enough for one day actually burned for eight days.

by which Jews recall their exodus from slavery. Many of the rituals involve eating special foods that remind Jews of certain aspects of the Passover story: bitter herbs recall the bitterness of slavery; sweet food recalls the sweetness of freedom; unleavened bread (called *matzah*) recalls that the Israelites left in such haste from Egypt that they didn't have time for their bread to rise. It is interesting to note that at a traditional seder, Moses' name is never mentioned. This striking absence is because the rabbis wished the full focus to be on God's redemption of Israel, and not the human agents God used for His mission.

Shavuout (usually in May) celebrates the day when the Israelites received God's laws at the foot of Mount Sinai.

Remembrance Days. Yom HaShoah (usually in April) is a day of Holocaust Remembrance. During World War II, Nazi Germany waged a war against the Jews. Hitler and his evil followers murdered two-thirds of all the Jews in Europe: 6 million Jews, of which 2 million were children. Nazism was the embodiment of evil in the world. Calling on centuries of anti-semitism, religious prejudice, and nationalistic racism, Nazis sought to manipulate their followers into blaming Jews for all their problems. Nazism was, in essence, the opposite of the Judeo-Christian code of morality. It supported legalized murder and tried to undo the religious notion that all humanity is created in the image of God.

Yom HaZikaron (April or May) is a Day of Remembrance for the Israeli soldiers who have died defending the land of Israel. The next day is Yom HaAtzma'ut, Israel's Independence Day. Declaring its independence on May 14, 1948, the Jewish homeland was formally recreated after 2,000 years of exile. Today, more than 25 percent of the world's Jews—more than 3 million people—live in Israel. Israel is the only country that grants any Jew in need the right to citizenship in a safe land, free of persecution.

Yom Yerushalyim (April or May) is the Day of Jerusalem. This holiday celebrates the reunification of Jerusalem under Israeli sovereignty. Until 1967, Jews were not allowed to pray at their holy sites, especially the Western Wall, the only remnant remaining from the original temple in Jerusalem. Today, Jerusalem is open to people of all religions.

Jewish Faith in America

While many modern American Jews vary in their religious knowledge and observance, most practicing Jews embrace the three major components of their faith. Those are a belief in God, an acceptance of the Torah as the Jewish blueprint for living God's laws, and the feeling that Jews are part of an ancient people with a rich spiritual and philosophical legacy. The Jewish heritage is rich, and while Judaism has remained a minority religion, the Judeo-Christian moral code permeates much of American intellectual history.

The American founders embraced the Bible as a foundation upon which to build the United States of America. American Jews played a role in contributing to the American evolution of democratic ideals and successes. More important, the Israelite moral legacy helped to create the bedrock of American democratic values.

Entering a Land of Opportunity

AMERICAN JEWS SHARE THEIR IMMIGRANT EXPERIENCE WITH MANY others who arrived on these shores. Like so many groups, they endured persecution, degradation, and poverty in their homelands, and they wanted something better. They were adventurous, hardworking, courageous people who dreamed of a better life for themselves and their families. Yet their history and traditions added an extra dimension to the experience. Early settlers in America relied heavily on their Bible to be a guide for daily living. And their Bible, the Old Testament, was, in fact, the Hebrew Bible—the Bible that both Christians and Jews believe God gave to the Jewish people. When all is said, it is this fact that defines the most significant contribution of the Jews to America.

The early Puritans recognized the Jews as "The People of the Book"— the people who had given this book, the Bible, to the world. Many of the democratic principles that govern American life are found in the words of the Bible. The Liberty Bell that stands on display in Independence Hall in Philadelphia is inscribed with a Biblical quotation: "Proclaim liberty throughout all the land unto all the inhabitants thereof." (Leviticus 25:10). And Thomas Jefferson may have looked to the Bible for inspiration when he wrote in the Declaration of Independence, "We hold these truths to be self-evident: that all men are created equal; that they are endowed by their Creator with certain inalienable rights; that among these are life, liberty, and the pursuit of happiness...."

Jefferson, along with the other Founding Fathers, were aware of and inspired by Biblical principles of justice and personal freedom. They were, however, careful not to make the same mistakes that had been made in Europe: that is, to establish one national religion. What set the United States apart was the Constitutional separation of church and state—effectively prohibiting the establishment of any particular religion as the national religion.

Is it fair to say that Jefferson's words were understood the same way in their time as we understand them now? Probably not. When Jefferson wrote, "all men are created equal," he did not include women or slaves; what he meant to say was that "all free men are created equal." Did the Declaration of Independence or the Constitution rule out the possibility that some states were, indeed, made up of people who mostly belonged to one particular religion? No. And did the Constitution guarantee that there would be no need for any further struggle for religious freedom? Certainly not. Indeed, the fight for individual rights under the law, as well as for civil rights, is one that continues even today. But fundamentally, the framers of the Constitution understood and valued personal freedom and sought to guarantee it to all citizens of the United States. What they understood was the spirit of the Biblical laws that had come from the Jews.

Throughout American history, Jews have played a significant role in working toward the ideals and principles that America was founded on. There were many Jewish patriots who fought and died in the American Revolution, and there were others who worked to finance the war effort. There were Jews who made a mark during the Civil War and the restoration that followed, and Jews who continue to support those ideals today.

Voyage to the New World

The story of American Jews begins in Spain in 1492, the very same year that Christopher Columbus sailed from Spain to find a new world. Earlier that year, on March 31, 1492, King Ferdinand had ordered all the Jews in Spain to either convert to Catholicism or leave the country by the end of July.

The Jews, who were called *sephardim*, had lived peacefully in

PRECEDING PAGE
Columbus' new world
It's likely some of the crew members on Christopher Columbus' famous voyage were Jews escaping the Spanish Inquisition. The artist of this 19th-century chromalith, First View of America, *is unknown.*

Spain for hundreds of years, serving various kings and queens, and contributing to the development of Spain as writers, philosophers, astronomers, and doctors. But in 1478, King Ferdinand ordered the beginning of an Inquisition, whose main goal was to create a united, Christian Spain. Despite the Inquisition, many Spanish Jews wanted to stay in Spain and Portugal. So to avoid the punishments of the Inquisition, they converted to Catholicism, and to the outside world they acted as Catholics. But at the same time, they lived as secret Jews. These Jews were called *conversos* or *marranos*.

Other Jews chose to leave Spain. Some historians think that some of the sailors who joined Columbus were Jewish. One important member of Columbus' crew was Luis de Torres, a *converso* who spoke Spanish, Hebrew, and some Arabic, making him a good choice to be an interpreter for Columbus.

Before Columbus left Spain, he found experts who would help him chart his course and assist him in obtaining funding for the journey. Among them were a good number of Jews, including Judah Cresques, who was the best mapmaker of his time, and Abraham Zacuto who was an astronomer and made navigational maps using the stars as his guide.

Arrival in the New World

Christopher Columbus set sail on August 3, 1492. His ships—the Pinta, the Niña, and the Santa Maria—reached land in October. The first place Columbus landed was on a small island in the Caribbean. Since Columbus had set out to reach Asia, he was disappointed and wanted to return to Spain. It was his interpreter, Luis de Torres, who encouraged Columbus to remain. Columbus did return to Spain, but he planned another exploration of the area where he had landed. And meanwhile, Torres had learned the language of the natives and made friends with them. One of them even offered him a piece of land and showed him how to smoke tobacco leaves.

Over the next century, Europeans continued to sail to the New World. The Portuguese first ruled in Brazil, but soon the Dutch took over that South American country. By the 1600s, Brazil became a destination for large numbers of *conversos*. The Dutch West India Company wanted to encourage people to settle in the New World, so they sent merchants to establish a harbor city named Recife, which means "city of reefs." Many of the *conversos* who settled in Recife managed farms and produced sugar. Living under Dutch rule, the *conversos* were again able to live as Jews without fear.

Soon, other Jews joined them and the city of Recife became a center for Jews. There they built synagogues, observed their holidays and customs, and built schools. But in 1654, the Portuguese won Recife back from the Dutch and, once again, the Jews were forced to leave.

And this is where the story of Jewish life in North America really begins. More than 150 families decided to leave Recife. Many sailed back to Holland, but some decided to extend their journey to the northern continent of the New World. They convinced the French captain of a ship called the Saint Catherine to take them, and promised him that their relatives would send the necessary money to pay him when they arrived in the Dutch colony of New Amsterdam.

New Amsterdam

After six long months at sea, 23 Jews arrived in New Amsterdam. The captain of the Saint Catherine immediately went to court, claiming that the Jews had not paid him for their voyage. The Jews told the judge that it was their intention to pay the captain in full and they would ask their relatives for more money. The judge placed some of the Jews in jail and confiscated the belongings of others. In addition, the court ruled that the Jewish immigrants would have to auction off whatever possessions they had in order to pay the debt.

This reception in New Amsterdam was neither welcoming nor warm. Governor Peter Stuyvesant (1592–1672) heard about the Jews on the Saint Catherine and immediately wrote to his employers at the Dutch West India Company to report the incident; he was determined to send these Jews away. His letter, written September 22, 1654, read, in part, "We have, for the benefit of this weak and newly developing place and the land in general, deemed it useful to require them [the Jews] in a friendly way to depart, so that the deceitful race be not allowed to further inflict and trouble this new colony to the detraction of your worships."

But the Jews also wrote to the Dutch West India Company. They reminded the directors of the company that they were loyal Dutch citizens. The directors of the Dutch West India Company received their letter and recognized that the information it contained was correct. In addition, many of the directors were, themselves, Jews. They told Gov-

An Answer From Amsterdam

From the Dutch West India Company to Peter Stuyvesant, April 26, 1655:

We would have liked to fulfill your wishes and request that the new territories should no more be allowed to be infected by people of the Jewish nation, for we foresee therefrom the same difficulties which you fear, but after having further weighed and considered the matter, we observe that this would be somewhat unreasonable and unfair, especially because of the considerable loss sustained by this nation, with others, in the taking of Brazil, and also because of the large amount of capital which they still have invested in the shares of this company. Therefore, after many deliberations we have finally decided and resolved to [agree to] a certain petition presented by said Portuguese Jews that these people may travel and trade to and in New Netherland and live and remain there, provided the poor among them shall not become a burden to the company or to the community, but be supported by their own nation. You shall now govern yourself accordingly.

ernor Stuyvesant that the Jews could stay in New Amsterdam.

Governor Stuyvesant did not expect such a reply from his employers. After receiving it, he did not stop trying to restrict the lives of the Jewish settlers. He prevented the Jews from building a synagogue, and from standing as guards for the settlement.

Asser Levy

The leader of the New Amsterdam Jewish community was Asser Levy (birth date unknown, died 1681), a successful businessman who traded furs with the Native Americans. To help alleviate the hardships placed on the Jewish community by Governor Stuyvesant, including an additional tax, and an ongoing struggle with Stuyvesant to allow them to trade with the Native Americans, open retail businesses, and worship in their traditional manner, Levy welcomed his Jewish neighbors to his home for Sabbath and holiday services and celebrations. Additionally, he opened a slaughterhouse where he refused to slaughter pigs.

While Governor Stuyvesant continued to place obstacles in their path, such as refusing to allow them to build a synagogue or buy land for a cemetery, to serve as guards, own real estate, or even become citizens, Levy organized his fellow Jews and insisted that they receive civil rights. Ultimately, they received the right not to appear in court on

Saturday (their Sabbath, when they were prohibited from doing any work or conducting business), and they received land for a Jewish cemetery. In about 10 years, the Jewish settlers owned their own land, served on guard duty, engaged in free trade, and became full citizens of the colony.

As leader of the Jewish community, Levy earned a reputation for being honest in business and for being generous. In addition to helping his own people, he was interested in assisting other members of the colony. When a group of Lutherans needed money to build their first church, Levy lent them the funds.

The example Levy set by insisting that Jews be granted their civil rights and that they maintain their own way of life set a standard that helped establish liberty for other minorities who would follow. Levy understood that his Jewish heritage, including the Bible, provided the basis for a democratic society promising religious freedom for its citizens.

By 1664, British armies conquered New Amsterdam and renamed it New York. The British granted the Jews even more freedom and eventually permitted them to build a synagogue. Construction of the first synagogue in North America thus began in 1728. Located on Mill Street in lower Manhattan, Congregation Shearith Israel (The Remnant of Israel) began its long and prestigious history.

Early struggle for rights
Asser Levy organized his fellow Jews in New Amsterdam to insist on their civil rights. Ultimately, they won the right to set up a synagogue and a cemetery, and to be regarded as equal citizens.

Other Colonial Settlements

Life in the four main early Jewish communities—New York, Newport, Philadelphia, and Savannah—revolved around similar patterns, and the new, democratic ideals of the British colonies helped to form their community organizations. Social action agencies were established alongside religious congregations to help those in need. The core Jewish values of *tzedakah* and *gemilut hasadim*—performing just acts (see chapter 4), and kindness—were essential to the makeup of these communities. Synagogues were built to hold schools, as well as houses of worship. Many Jews became successful businessmen, merchants, traders, community activists, and leaders in their new home cities.

Trade among the colonies and with other countries was good business for the Jews. They could depend on family members and friends who were in the same business, and they could rely on their contacts to be honest businessmen. This led to many a combined venture and, ultimately, to the building of strong networks of mutual benefit.

Newport, Rhode Island. Roger Williams (1604–1684), an outspoken minister who had been sent away from Massachusetts by the Puritans, founded the colony of Rhode Island in 1636. He believed that freedom of worship should be extended to all citizens. The Puritans were certainly influenced by the Jews. They had embraced ideas from the Jewish Bible, and compared themselves to the ancient Israelites who were freed from Egyptian slavery. Many of their laws were based on laws found in the Bible. They used Biblical names for their children, insisted on a knowledge of the Hebrew language and made it a requirement at both Harvard and Yale, and modeled their harvest holiday of Thanksgiving after the Festival of Sukkot (see page 16). Still, they were not tolerant of anyone who did not agree with their religious views. Williams found it remarkable that while the Puritans themselves had come to America in search of religious freedom, they were not as eager to share their colony with others who had different religious ideas.

The first Jews arrived in the port city of Newport, Rhode Island, in 1755, after an earthquake in Portugal. Making use of their contacts with other Jews in other places, men such as Jacob Rivera (1717–1789) and Aaron Lopez (1731–1782) became very successful businessmen, importing goods from Europe to Newport, then shipping the goods to other port cities along the East Coast. Lopez alone owned about 30 ships that brought different kinds of fine cloth, tea, soap, and other luxury items to the American colonies. In addition, Lopez, Rivera, and Hart owned factories where candles were made from a byproduct of whale oil. Many English families bought candles made in Newport. Other items sent back to Europe included fur, dried fish, sugar, and rice. Jewish-owned businesses in Newport made soap, silver, and brass products.

In 1759, with assistance from members of Congregation Shearith Israel in New York, ground was broken for the first synagogue in Newport. This became known as the Touro Synagogue. It was completed in 1763, and remains the oldest standing synagogue in the United States. It is interesting to note that the builders of the synagogue included a trap door under the reader's desk that led to an escape tunnel. With memories of the Spanish Inquisition still vivid, it is possible they were not totally convinced that the liberties promised them by the new government would remain in force. The secret tunnel would eventually be used as a stop on the Underground Railroad during the Civil War.

Philadelphia, Pennsylvania. The colony of Pennsylvania was given to William Penn (1644–1718) in payment of a debt owed him by King Charles II of England. Penn, a Quaker, seized the opportunity to welcome members of his religion to a better place, because the Quakers had been among the persecuted in England.

Philadelphia, called the City of Brotherly Love, is located on the Delaware River, making it an ideal location for traders to exchange their goods. Flatboats, canoes, and rafts were used to transport furs traded from Native Americans to Boston, New York, and Newport. In return, similar kinds of boats would return with sugar, coffee, housewares, fish, and other items. Merchants would load the provisions onto horse-drawn wagons to reach their final destinations. In most instances, Jews were both the traders and the suppliers of these shipments.

Barnard (1738–1801) and Michael Gratz (1740–1811) were among the most successful merchants in pre-Revolutionary Philadelphia. Together with Joseph Simon (1712–1804), they founded and funded Mikveh Israel, the first Jewish congregation in Philadelphia. Born in Central Europe, the Gratz brothers come to Philadelphia by way of London. Shortly after their arrival, they began their careers as merchants and traders, concentrating their efforts along the East Coast from Canada to the West Indies. Before and during the Revolutionary War, the Gratz

A Letter From the President

In 1790, one year after the inauguration of George Washington as the first president of the United States, the members of the Jewish community in Newport sent him a letter expressing their affection for the new president and welcoming him on his visit to Newport. They wrote, "Deprived as we have hitherto been of the invaluable rights of free citizens, we now, with a deep sense of gratitude to the Almighty Disposer of all events, behold a government, erected by the majority of the people, a government which to bigotry gives no sanction, to persecution no assistance, but generously affording to all liberty of conscience and immunities of citizenship, deeming every one, of whatever nation, tongue or language, equal parts of the great governmental machine. This so ample and extensive federal union whose basis is philanthropy, mutual confidence, and public virtue, we cannot but acknowledge to be the work of the great God, who ruleth in the armies of heaven and among the inhabitants of the earth, doing whatsoever seemeth him good."

Washington responded, "It would be inconsistent with the frankness of my character not to avow that I am pleased with your favorable opinion of my administration and fervent wishes for my felicity. May the children of the stock of Abraham who dwell in this land continue to merit and enjoy the good will of the other inhabitants, while every one shall sit in safely under his own vine and fig tree, and there shall be none to make him afraid. May the Father of all mercies scatter light and not darkness in our paths, and make us all in our several vocations useful here, and, in his own due time and way, everlastingly happy."

brothers remained loyal to the American side. They signed the Non-Importation Resolutions, pledging not to import British-made goods until the Stamp Act was repealed. (The Stamp Act was initiated in 1765 by Prime Minister George Grenville to raise additional money to pay for food and shelter for British military forces. Special tax stamps were required to be placed on a variety of items, including commercial and legal documents, newspapers, marriage licenses, playing cards, and other items that were traded.)

Following the war, Barnard ventured west to Pittsburgh to negotiate a treaty with the Native Americans, and to procure land grants, which led to a major expansion of the family business.

Savannah, Georgia. In the early 1700s, a large portion of London's citizens lived in terrible poverty. People who owed money were regularly sent to prison, where they sometimes remained for the rest of their lives. The prisons were getting overcrowded with debtors. James Oglethorpe (1696–1785), a member of the British Parliament, proposed a solution to the king: transport the prisoners to America. A colony in

A place to worship

Building a synagogue was one of the most important tasks of any Jewish community. This synagogue was built in Philadelphia in the 1800s by the Spanish and Portuguese Congregation of Mikveh Israel.

the southern part of America would serve as a buffer between British settlements in the north, the Spanish settlement of Florida, and the French settlements to the west. The king liked Oglethorpe's idea, and in 1733, taking more than 100 debtors from London jails, Oglethorpe began his journey to establish a new colony.

Large numbers of Jewish refugees from all over Europe had also arrived in London, creating a heavy burden on the established Jewish community. Bevis Marks, a leader of the Jewish community, was aware of Oglethorpe's plan and organized the leadership of the Jewish community to contribute funds to Oglethorpe's venture. Seeing his plan as a solution to their own problem, they arranged for and financed another ship to sail to the new colony, and thus Jews arrived in the colony of Savannah shortly after the original group of British settlers.

In Georgia, the English trustees attempted to limit the number of Jews. However, Oglethorpe had already granted them the privileges of citizens. In the end, the trustees prevailed by limiting the Jews' ability to engage in commerce and by refusing to allow them to own slaves. Within nine years of their arrival, most of the Jewish settlers left Savannah, moving north to the thriving port city of Charleston, South Carolina.

Benjamin (1692–1765) and Perla Sheftall were among the passengers on the ship carrying Jewish settlers to Savannah. Their arrival marked yet another first for Jewish immigrants: They were *ashkenaz-*

im, Jews from northern and eastern Europe. The *sephardim* regarded these *ashkenazim* as less observant Jews, and were less than willing to accept the *ashkenazim* into their congregations.

The Revolutionary War

The British government saw their colonies in America as a potential source of income to help pay the huge debt that had built up following years of war. It never considered that the colonists might resist all this taxation, but their opposition to the taxes proved to be strong. Still, the taxes kept piling up. In April 1775, the American Revolution began.

At the beginning of the war, approximately 2,000 Jews were living in the colonies. While many of them remained loyal to the British, those who fought with the colonists made significant contributions. Some Jewish merchants, including the Gratz brothers from Philadelphia, signed the Non-Importation Resolutions. When the British captured New York City in 1776, Jewish merchants, including Jonas Philips (d.1807), Isaac Moses (1741/2–1818) Hayman Levy (1721–1789), Robert Morris (1733–1806), Myer Myers (1723–1795) and Aaron Lopez, left New York and spent the war in Philadelphia, where they enlisted in the militia and aided the war effort. Meyers, a silversmith, melted metal household items into bullets; Moses provided supplies to the Continental Army.

Men like Francis Salvador (1747–1776) of South Carolina, and Mordecai Sheftall (1735–1797) of Georgia risked their own lives and fortunes for the sake of American Independence. Benjamin Sheftall, who had established a shipping business and a series of warehouses along the Savannah wharf, would stand on the docks and refuse to allow British captains to unload their cargo. He was soon appointed to the staff of the Georgia Brigade, where he served as a quartermaster, and shortly after that he was given the responsibility of supplying food and clothing to the Continental troops of South Carolina and Georgia. Captured by the British, Sheftall refused to reveal American secrets. He and his son were imprisoned, but were later released in an exchange for British prisoners of war.

Westward Expansion

By the early 1800s, the number of immigrants coming to the United States swelled, and many of the new arrivals moved westward, where vast tracts of undeveloped land awaited. The promise of freedom,

ASHKENAZIM
From the Hebrew word *ashkenaz*, which means "Germany," *ashkenazim* are Jews who come from northern and eastern Europe.

together with unparalleled opportunities for growth and wealth, further encouraged immigration to American shores.

In Europe, Jews had been forced into tiny ghettos for hundreds of years. They had been denied citizenship, civil rights, education, and the opportunity to enter many professions. They were poor and tired of persecution. Beginning in 1815, after Napoleon's defeat at Waterloo, a major wave of Jewish immigrants arrived in America. Most often, the men came first, alone. They hoped to find employment and save enough to bring their families. Arriving in seaport cities, they quickly learned that the West offered more promise. And so they went. Tailors, cobblers, peddlers of old clothes, and other unskilled workers packed up their wagons and headed toward the Ohio Valley and beyond. They settled in small towns in Tennessee, Ohio, Missouri, Minnesota, Louisiana, Colorado, and Texas, mostly opening small shops. As in other established Jewish communities, they acquired land for their synagogues and cemeteries.

When gold was discovered in California in 1848, the Gold Rush towns of the West Coast became the destination of choice.

Levi Strauss (1829–1902) followed the gold seekers. Carrying burlap, a heavy, plain-woven fabric, in his wagon, he tried to sell this strong material to the gold miners. However, it wasn't until he teamed up with a tailor that he found success. The burlap was sewn into pants that were strong enough to endure the rough life of the miners, the pockets were secured with copper rivets, and a business was born. Strauss used his first name, Levi, as the name for these pants. From one bolt of burlap, factories manufacturing "Levi jeans" grew into a worldwide brand.

Slavery and the Civil War

While the move westward drew thousands of immigrants, serious trouble was brewing in the South. Capitalizing on profits from growing cotton, indigo (a clothing dye), and tobacco, many southern plantation owners grew enormously wealthy. But their wealth was built on the cheap labor of slaves imported from Africa. Slavery was an accepted fact of life from the time the first colonies were established in America. But over time, views changed, and eventually, the country divided over this issue. In the South, slaves were considered property, not human beings. While there were some Jews who owned plantations and slaves,

ANOTHER KIND OF PATRIOT

Haym Solomon (1740–1785) made financial contributions to the war effort that were, in their own way, as heroic as any soldier's. Born in Poland, Solomon spent many years traveling through Europe. His dream, however, was to come to America. Arriving in New York at the beginning of the Revolution, Solomon was quickly captured by the British and arrested on suspicion of being a spy. He was able to escape, with assistance from his family and friends, and fled to Philadelphia. There he went into business as a broker, eventually joining Robert Morris in the Continental Office of Finance. Morris assigned Solomon to serve as treasurer, with the principle task of raising funds for loans to the revolutionary government. In his position as broker, Solomon used much of his own money to support the American fight for liberty.

the vast majority of Jews did not because they believed slavery was wrong.

Judah P. Benjamin (1811–1884), a *sephardic* Jew who had become a successful Louisiana lawyer and plantation owner, took an active role in the Confederacy and led the pro-slavery forces. When floodwaters forced him to sell his plantation and all of his slaves, he turned to a career in politics and was elected a senator from Louisiana. When the Southern states seceded from the Union in 1861, he resigned his Senate seat and joined Jefferson Davis' cabinet, where he served as both secretary of war and secretary of state. After the war, Benjamin fled to England, where he became a highly respected lawyer.

Rabbi Morris Raphall (1798–1868) of New York delivered sermons claiming that slavery was not sinful. However, he encouraged slave owners to treat their slaves with kindness and to recognize that they were human beings. But these two men were a minority among Jews.

Most Jews spoke out against slavery. Rabbi David Einhorn of Baltimore (1809–1879) was one of many outspoken advocates for the abolition of slavery. Einhorn was warned that if he continued to speak out against slavery, his life and the lives of his family members would be

Serving with distinction
Lt. Col. Israel Moses (1821–1870) was an officer and a military surgeon who served in Mexico and later in the Civil War. He also founded a hospital in New York.

in danger. So he moved his family to Philadelphia and then returned to Baltimore, where he continued his campaign against slavery. Einhorn was adamant about his anti-slavery activities and called on Jews to prepare themselves to wage war against it.

Ernestine Rose (1810–1892) was another outspoken abolitionist. Her speeches were well-attended in New York, where she was known as the "Queen of Platforms." During the Civil War, she, along with other influential women, collected signatures in support of President Abraham Lincoln's Emancipation Proclamation. In 1850, she began to speak out in favor of granting women the right to vote, and in 1869 she helped to organize the Women's Suffrage Society.

Once again, Jews from all over the country took up arms in defense of their country. Approximately 7,000 Jews fought for the Union and 3,000 for the Confederacy. Elias Leon Hyneman served as a sergeant of the 5th Pennsylvania Cavalry, fighting in the Battle of Bull Run, Gettysburg, and the Battle of the Wilderness. Known for going behind enemy lines, he often found himself assisting wounded soldiers. He was eventually captured and imprisoned.

Other Jewish soldiers also distinguished themselves. Max Sachs, a lieutenant in Company C of the 32nd Infantry, single-handedly held back the enemy in Bowling Green, Kentucky. Benjamin Levy was only a teenager when he enlisted as a drummer-boy in the 1st New York Volunteers, and as the war progressed, he distinguished himself as a courageous soldier. And Edward Solomon was promoted to the rank of Major for his bravery in the 24th Illinois Infantry.

In 1861, Congress passed a law saying that every regiment in the Union Army was required to have a Christian chaplain. A delegation of Jews wrote to President Lincoln, as well as to legislators in both houses, requesting that rabbis be included to serve Jewish soldiers. The president agreed, and in 1862 the law was amended to include clergy of all religions to serve as chaplains. Rabbi Jacob Frankel (1808–1887) was the first rabbi to be appointed an army chaplain.

Despite all of the acts of courage shown by Jewish soldiers on both sides of the Mason-Dixon Line during the Civil War, there were incidents that greatly harmed the Jewish population in America. It seemed as though the anti-Semitic feelings that had been so strong in Europe had now crossed the ocean. In the North, when it appeared that the war was going badly, General Ulysses S. Grant (1822–1885) issued Order No. 11 that stated: "The Jews, as a class violating every regulation of trade established by the Treasury Department and also department orders, are hereby expelled from the department within twenty-four hours from receipt of this order." To his credit, President Lincoln received a delegation of Jews from Kentucky, listened to their complaint of unfair treatment, and acted quickly to revoke the order. Similarly, in the South, many Jews were blamed for supply shortages and high prices. Jews were blamed because they were so heavily involved in supplies and shipping, but there was no real evidence of wrongdoing by Jewish businessmen.

In the years that followed the Civil War, America's Jews understood better than many that the deep divisions had to be healed. A core value of all Jewish communities is, "All Jews are responsible for one another." This idea was expanded to include all Americans. Helping one another with acts of kindness would help the country heal.

A CALL TO ARMS

Rabbi Samuel Isaacs (1804–1878), a staunch supporter of President Abraham Lincoln, wrote the following editorial in the December 28, 1860, issue of *The Jewish Messenger*. in response to the call for volunteers to defend the Union: "Then stand by the flag!...Whether native or foreign born, Christian or Israelite, stand by it, and you are doing your duty, and acting well your part on the side of liberty and justice! We know full well that our young men, who have left their homes to respond to the call of their country, will render a good account for themselves. We have no fears for their bravery and patriotism. Our prayers are with them. God speed them on the work which they have volunteered to perform!"

2

Judaism Adapts in America

REPRESSION, POVERTY, AND PERSECUTION LED JEWS TO FLEE
Europe. Kings, czars, and other political leaders forced Jews to live in ghettos, denied them their civil rights and opportunities for education and employment, and subjected them to persecution. Jews were humiliated and subjected to violence because they were considered enemies of Christianity.

There were times when a more relaxed, tolerant position was taken toward Jews, but these periods were rare. For example, in 1844, as part of a de-
cree that established Jewish schools in Russia, the Russian government declared, "The purpose of educating the Jews is to bring about their gradual
merging with the Christian nationalities, and to uproot those superstitions
and harmful prejudices which are instilled by the teachings of the Talmud."

Life in America provided hope. Jewish immigrants found opportunities to prosper and to fulfill their ambitions and dreams. America provided
a safe haven to create, to build, and to flourish. Today, the United States is
home to the largest and most influential community of Jews outside Israel.

Immigration from Germany

The opening of the American frontier coincided with political upheaval in
Europe, particularly in Germany, which was undergoing a period of

confederation. The unrest in Europe was the essential cause of a massive wave of immigration to America, and large numbers of Jews were among the immigrants. While many Jews settled in the East Coast cities, more were attracted to the West with its tales of adventure and opportunities for financial success.

Most of the Jews on the frontier were peddlers, merchants, and traders. However, there were also some doctors, lawyers, judges, and government officials. What they shared was a common dream—to become Americans—and to achieve this goal, they established similar patterns of growth and development. After setting up shops to sell household necessities, sewing supplies, "dry goods," and other retail items, they would buy land in or near the town for a cemetery, organize a congregation, and, as their numbers grew and members prospered, they would build a synagogue, establish schools, and create mutual benefit organizations.

As businesses grew, many German Jewish shop owners recognized the need to expand the types of items they sold. Some, like Levi Strauss, became clothing manufacturers, employing tailors and salesmen who laid the groundwork for an American ready-to-wear clothing industry. A few very successful shop owners moved back to Philadelphia and New York City to open department stores such as Bloomingdale's, Sears Roebuck, and Macy's. German Jewish peddlers and shop owners founded all three of these stores, and others like them. Some immigrants opened factories where uniforms for the American Army were mass-produced in standard sizes. And, to address the needs of those living in remote areas of the plains or the prairies, some German Jewish immigrants developed mail-order businesses.

The discovery of gold in California added to the attraction of the West. Jews, too, joined the Gold Rush in search of their fortune. In 1849, two synagogues were established in San Francisco: one to accommodate German Jews and the other for Polish Jews. When gold was discovered in Arizona, Jews set up shops in Phoenix and Tombstone to supply the miners. Among the businessmen who achieved success in Arizona were Michael and Joseph Goldwater. Michael Goldwater (1820s–1903) was the grandfather of Arizona senator and presidential candidate Barry Goldwater (1909–1998).

German Jews who immigrated to the United States in the 1800s contributed to the secularization of American Jewish life. A strong cultural attachment to German customs linked many of the German Jewish immigrants. Frustrated with their inability to connect with the already established *sephardic* community, these immigrants needed to learn English and practice the customs of their new country. Wanting to retain their Jewish identity, they found security in separating themselves from the older, established Jewish congregations and forming new ones to address their needs. At the same time, they established fraternal organizations that supported core Jewish values but expressed them in terms of social and political activism, rather than religious services. The National Council of Jewish Women and B'nai Brith, for example, were organized to facilitate the Americanization process and later evolved to address issues of national concern.

Wealthy German Jewish families, including the Guggenheims, Warburgs, Schiffs, Strauses, Kahns, Altmans, and others, became patrons of the arts and education, donating generously to libraries, orchestras, museums, and universities.

Immigration from Eastern Europe

More than 2.5 million Eastern European Jews immigrated to the United States between 1881 and 1914. In Russia, 1881 was a turning point for Jews; everything that went wrong there was blamed on them, including the assassination of Czar Alexander II. The poverty of the peasants, poor crop yields, and even political unrest was blamed on the Jews. Russian leaders organized mobs of peasants to participate in riots, called pogroms, to eliminate the Jews from society. The situation was so bad that 1881 was dubbed "Year of the Pogrom."

In 1882, the May Laws were enacted in Russia to force Jews to leave their villages and move to cities. In 1905, large numbers of Russians rose in revolt against the Czar. The revolt was crushed, and violent pogroms spread to the cities. With no available housing and their businesses destroyed, millions of Jews made their way to the United States.

New York's Lower East Side

The Jews who sailed across the Atlantic Ocean in this wave of immigration were mostly very poor; they traveled in steerage class—the cheapest passage available on steamships. For most, the first glimpse of America was the Statue of Liberty in New York Harbor. In 1903, a sonnet written by a Jewish woman, Emma Lazarus (1849–1887), was inscribed

FIND OUT MORE
The Museum of American Jewish History in Philadelphia (www.nmajh.org) is devoted to chronicling the experience of American Jews through its exhibitions—both permanent and traveling—educational programs, and on-line information.

The New Colossus
by Emma Lazarus, 1883

Not like the brazen giant of Greek fame,
With conquering limbs astride from land to land;
Here at our sea-washed, sunset gates shall stand
A mighty woman with a torch, whose flame
Is the imprisoned lightning, and her name
Mother of Exiles. From her beacon-hand
Glows world-wide welcome; her mild eyes command
The air-bridged harbor that twin cities frame.
"Keep, ancient lands, your storied pomp!" cries she
With silent lips. "Give me your tired, your poor,
Your huddled masses yearning to breathe free,
The wretched refuse of your teeming shore.
Send these, the homeless, tempest-tossed to me.
I lift my lamp beside the golden door."

on a tablet placed at the pedestal of Lady Liberty. Lazarus' poem, *The New Colossus*, expressed the hopes and dreams of all immigrants.

Coming off the ship in New York, all the immigrants in steerage class were taken directly to Ellis Island, where immigration officials registered them and gave them physical examinations. The officials did not always understand the immigrants' languages, so their names were sometimes changed or misspelled. Those who were admitted were taken by ferry to Battery Park in lower Manhattan, where their life in America began. Traveling north from Battery Park, they were often able to find "landsmen," people who had come from the same town or village, shared the same customs and religious practices, and spoke the same language—Yiddish.

Many immigrants arrived with the expectation that America was the *Goldeneh Medinah*, the "golden land." They were sorely disappointed and shocked to find that the streets of New York's Lower East Side were definitely not paved with gold! Arriving penniless and as unskilled workers, many of the immigrants were forced to live in overcrowded tenement apartments. Work was obtained either in unsanitary, dangerous sweatshops, where they were paid by the piece to cut, sew, or press items of clothing, or in factories, where they would roll tobacco into cigars.

Uptown vs. Downtown Jews

Sharp social distinctions emerged between the established "uptown Jews," Jews of German descent who, because of their wealth and involvement in politics, had assimilated into American society; and the "downtown Jews," newcomers from Eastern European countries, who

The new ghetto
Jewish neighborhoods, such as New York's Orchard Street in the 1890s, often resembled the old European ghettos. The difference was that with hard work, Jews could leave the poor life behind.

were uneducated and poor. The German uptown Jews had already organized and virtually controlled Jewish communal life; they were successful businessmen and they had penetrated Christian social circles.

However, with the arrival of millions of the Eastern European Jews, they feared the possibility that their friendly Christian associates might once again begin to see Jews as "foreigners." They quickly organized settlement houses, schools, and community centers whose goal was to Americanize the new immigrants—teach them English and American customs, provide job training, and prepare them to become American citizens.

The Jewish Daily Forward

Often separated from family and bewildered by life in America, thousands of immigrants wrote to the offices of *The Jewish Daily Forward*, a Yiddish-language newspaper founded in 1897, which helped bring familiarity and comfort to Jewish immigrants.

In a column called "The Bintel Brief" (A Bundle of Letters), immigrants of all ages would pour out their hearts in search of advice. The following letter is quoted in the 1971 book *A Bintel Brief* by Harry Golden and Isaac Metzker.

Dear Editor, I am a newsboy, 14 years old, and I sell the Forverts *in the street till late into the nights. I come to you to ask your advice. I was born in Russia and was 12 years old when I came to America with my dear mother. My sister, who was in the country before us, brought us over.*

My sister worked and supported us. She didn't allow me to go to work but sent me to school. I went to school for two years and didn't miss a day. But then came the terrible fire at the triangle shop, where she worked, and I lost my dear sister. My mother and I suffer terribly from

the misfortune. I had to help my mother and after school hours I go out and sell newspapers.

I have to go to school three more years, and after that I want to go to college. But my mother doesn't want me to go to school because she thinks I should go to work. I tell her I will work days and study at night but she won't hear of it. Since I read the Forverts *to my mother every night and read the answers to The Bintel Brief, I beg you to answer me and say a few words to her. Your reader, The Newsboy*

The answer to this letter is directed to the boy's mother, whose daughter was one of the shop workers who perished in the Triangle Shirtwaist Company fire on March 25, 1911. The woman is comforted for her loss, and is then told that she must not hinder her son's nighttime studies, but must help him reach his goal. And an appeal is made to people who may be able to help the boy further his education to come forward.

Many people would respond to pleas such as this one, doing all they could to help fellow Jews.

Among the communal organizations established to deal with the large numbers of immigrants was the Hebrew Immigrant Aid Society (HIAS). Formed in 1909, after merging with other agencies whose mission was to assist new immigrants, HIAS sent Yiddish-speaking representatives to Ellis Island to assist the arriving immigrants, then help them find housing, food, and jobs.

The Reform Movement

The central question challenging both the German and the Eastern European Jews was how to respond to the realities of modern life and maintain their identity as Jews. Many young intellectuals felt that the only way to avoid the conflict between traditional Judaism and modernity, and between acceptance into society and the violence of anti-Semitism in Europe, was to convert to Christianity. Jewish leaders hoped to reverse this trend by modernizing and liberalizing Jewish practices. They were deeply concerned about the future of Judaism and the Jewish people. This was the beginning of Reform Judaism.

The first reformers were Germans, although, ultimately, the Reform movement had its greatest impact in the United States. They were interested in making aesthetic changes to the manner of praying; they introduced German translations of the prayers and conducted the services in a more formal manner. Until this time, all prayers had been in Hebrew. But many people could no longer read or understand Hebrew. As German citizens, they spoke German, and they wanted their rabbi to deliver his weekly sermon in German. They also wanted a shorter service, prayers translated into German, musical accompaniment for the cantor, and a choir to enhance the beauty of the service.

While lay leaders took these first steps, the ideological changes that followed emerged as a result of a series of conferences among a group of rabbis and scholars who, in addition to their ordination as rabbis, had completed secular studies at major universities. Feeling that many of the ancient teachings found in the Talmud were no longer relevant to modern life, they looked more closely to the Bible and to secular scholarship to justify liberalizing the observance of the Sabbath and the holidays.

Ultimately, the most radical change adopted by the reformers was the rejection of the legally binding authority of *halakhah* (Jewish law), and of the belief that God had literally revealed the Torah at

A meeting of reformers
The organizers of the Jewish Reformed movement. Isaac Mayer Wise, the first Reform rabbi in the United States, is seated in the center.

Mount Sinai. According to the reformers, only those laws that deal with ethical aspects of human life (for example, how we are to treat animals, the environment, and other people), are considered to be binding. And the Torah, they said, was clearly written by men with divine inspiration. By rejecting God's direct authorship of the Torah, they also rejected the requirement to follow the kosher dietary laws, strict observance of the Sabbath, and other laws.

What the reformers retained was the belief in one God. They stressed the importance of ethics and social action as a way of expressing this belief. While respecting the traditions and heritage of those who preceded them, they encouraged each Jew to make personal choices as to which laws to follow.

Reform Judaism made its formal debut in America in 1840, when Rabbi Isaac Mayer Wise (1819–1900) began teaching the new ideas to his congregation in Albany, New York. Unfortunately, the congregation did not respond well to the changes he introduced—especially the president of the congregation, Louis Spanier, who, in a moment of rage, punched the rabbi. After considering his options, Rabbi Wise relocated to Cincinnati, Ohio, where he became the single most influential person shaping American Reform Judaism.

Among the innovative changes he introduced were organ music

in services, family pews instead of the traditional seating that separated men and women, holding Friday evening services after sunset to encourage families to attend together, and preaching the sermon in English. In addition, Wise introduced a new prayer book called *Minhag America*, hoping it would become a standard for all American Jews.

Above all else, the Reform movement in America emphasized the personal freedom of the individual. Central to the teachings of Reform Judaism is that all Jews have the right to make up their own minds about how to be Jewish. As Americans, the reformers believed that personal freedom was a natural human right.

In 1850, there were four Reform congregations in the United States. By 1873, 34 Reform congregations voted to create an umbrella organization called the Union of American Congregations. And in 1875, the Hebrew Union College opened its doors in Cincinnati as a seminary to train American rabbis to serve the Reform movement.

One of the most dramatic, and unsuccessful, changes made by the American reformers was changing the observance of the Sabbath from Saturday to Sunday. But Reform Judaism has continued to evolve and change. By 1880, more than 90 percent of American synagogues were affiliated with the Reform movement.

Conservative Judaism

At the same time that the early reformers were at work in Germany, Rabbi Zechariah Frankel (1801–1875) was serving as chief rabbi of Dresden, Germany. Frankel had not attended the first Reform rabbinical conference, but had criticized the conclusions reached by the participants. He decided to attend the second conference in the hope that he would be able to have some effect on the discussions. But he so strongly disagreed with the direction of the reforms, that he left.

The issue Frankel felt so strongly about was the use of Hebrew as the language of Jewish prayer. While Frankel agreed that German should be included in the liturgy, he also felt Hebrew deserved its rightful place. He argued that Hebrew had been the unifying language for the Jewish people for more than 2,000 years.

Frankel wanted his colleagues to consider the weight of history and tradition before making radical changes to the way people practice Judaism. He wanted to develop a way of understanding the beliefs and practices of Judaism that would be consistent with modern methods of

KEEPING KOSHER

Known as the laws of *kashrut*, the collection of dietary laws found in the Torah outlines what foods can and cannot be eaten, and how these foods must be prepared. Food that conforms to the *kashrut* is often described as kosher, which means "fitting, correct."

The laws of *kashrut* include a list of animals that may not be eaten, rules about how to slaughter animals for food, a prohibition against eating the blood of any animal, which parts of an animal may not be eaten, a prohibition against eating meat and dairy products together, and rules about how meat and dairy products and utensils must be separated.

Why do Jews observe the laws of *kashrut*? Because they believe God commanded them to do so. Many rabbis have explained that the dietary laws are also designed to help Jews distinguish between what is holy and what is not.

investigation and that would be based on a community who would accept them. He pointed out that throughout history, Jewish beliefs and practices were dynamic; they changed according to time and location.

Frankel called on his colleagues to join him to form another response to modernity. They formed what came to be known as the Conservative movement.

While both the Reform and Conservative movements began in Germany, their development in America took very different paths. The first American reformers were German immigrants who had already begun to make changes in their practice of Judaism when they founded their seminary. The Conservative movement began with the creation of a school to train rabbis to serve American congregations. Founded in 1887, the Jewish Theological Seminary of America adopted a curriculum that applied academic methods to the study of classical Jewish texts—particularly the Talmud and codes of Jewish law—together with courses in the Bible, Jewish history, literature, philosophy, practical aspects of preaching, and the Hebrew language.

Men applying to the Jewish Theological Seminary would have to be graduates of a secular undergraduate university. Rabbi Sabato Morais (1823–1897) was appointed the first president.

Traditional observance translated into an American expression seemed to fit perfectly with the goals of the Conservative leaders and also met the needs of the Eastern European immigrants. When they arrived in the United States, these immigrants desperately needed to hold on to a traditional way of life that had sustained them in their isolated small towns.

Early leaders of the Conservative movement supported the idea of "enlightened traditionalism." They felt that while much of the traditional package of Jewish beliefs and practices had to be retained, much needed to be changed. They expressed a willingness to adopt a more modern, critical, and open approach to the study of Judaism.

Raising the funds to support the Jewish Theological Seminary proved to be a difficult task, but the Conservative movement received the support and financial backing from a surprising source: leaders of the Reform movement. Through the networking efforts of Cyrus Adler (1863–1940), a student of Rabbi Sabato Morais, a group of wealthy Reform Jews raised more than $500,000 and recruited an internationally renowned scholar of rabbinical studies at Oxford University in England, Solomon Schechter (1847–1915), to be the leader of the Seminary. It was Schechter who shaped the future of both the Seminary and the Conservative movement.

Under Schechter's leadership, the Seminary attracted a top faculty and earned a reputation for excellence in advanced Jewish studies. Schechter is also credited with creating the congregational organization of the Conservative movement: the United Synagogue of America.

According to Schechter, "Unless we succeed in effecting an organization which, while loyal to the Torah, to the teachings of our sages, to the traditions of our fathers, to the usage and customs of Israel, shall at the same time introduce the English sermon, and adopt scientific methods in our seminaries, and bring order and decorum to our synagogues, traditional Judaism will not survive another century in this country."

Schechter believed that Judaism had the resources to deal with modern life, and that it would emerge strengthened and enriched. Schechter's goal was to create a center that would adapt scientific methods to the study of Bible and Talmud. He wanted to compare Jewish religious forms with those of other religions and cultures. He also wanted to be able to accept the fact that Judaism was influenced by the conditions of the community outside the Jewish world.

Schechter also demanded the democratization of the Jewish authority structure, that is, to let the people have more of a voice. This was a demand that was bound to cause tension. He firmly believed that a community of knowledgeable, caring Jews could and would serve as a deciding body for the Jewish community.

Conservative Judaism offered, and continues to offer, a mix of classical Judaism and contemporary American ways of thinking. Conservative Judaism has become the movement advocating both tradition and change. As the movement has grown, its members have displayed a variety of beliefs and practices, continuing the struggle between past and present, ancient and modern.

Conservative Jews recognize the authority of Jewish law (halakhah) and the impact of the law on the community of believers. The community is led by rabbinical scholars, who determine when change and adaptation are needed. Their prayer book, used on the Sabbath and holidays, includes the familiar prayers with the original Hebrew text

THE TALMUD

Compiled in Babylon and in Jerusalem, the Talmud contains a collection of interpretations of the laws found in the Torah. The Talmud is made of a philosophical legal code, called the Mishnah, and an extensive analysis and commentary upon the Mishnah, called the Gemara. It is divided into six sections to interpret laws pertaining to agriculture; Sabbath and holidays; marriage, divorce and other contracts; tort laws and other financial laws; sacrifices and the Temple; and ritual purity and impurity.

and English translations, familiar melodies, and a shortened service. Men and women sit together in the synagogue.

The Reconstructionist Movement

Created as an offshoot of the Conservative movement, Reconstructionist Judaism offered a radical new re-interpretation and direction to American Jews. Its prime mover was Mordecai Kaplan (1881–1983), a rabbi born in Russia and educated in the United States. Ordained at the Jewish Theological Seminary, Kaplan served as an assistant rabbi at a prominent Orthodox synagogue in New York. Uncomfortable with the practices and philosophies of that synagogue and of Orthodoxy, Kaplan joined the faculty of the Seminary, where he created the Teachers Institute.

At the Seminary, Kaplan was a demanding professor, asking hard, probing questions about religion: What makes a religion true, or false? What is God? What do we, as Jews, believe? He led his students in an investigation into the phenomenon of religion as a human activity.

Ultimately, Kaplan concluded that all religion is true, because the community of believers has made it true. The result of Kaplan's work was an important book, *Judaism as a Civilization*, in which he claimed that Judaism is more than a religion. Kaplan said Judaism includes more than beliefs and practices; it includes a language, history, art, music, and a sense of belonging—making it totally and completely accessible to all Jews, regardless of their background. Kaplan's Judaism was an evolving religious community that gave meaning to everyday life.

Among the innovations Kaplan introduced to American Jewish life was the *bat mitzvah*. Previously, only boys had marked their coming of age in a celebration called *bar mitzvah* (see page 15). His daughter, Judith, was the first Jewish young woman to celebrate a *bat mitzvah*.

By 1963, it was clear that Kaplan's Reconstructionist ideas could no longer make their home in the Conservative movement. The leadership of the Seminary, the Rabbinical Assembly, and the United Synagogue officially voted to reject Kaplan's changes. Kaplan took his followers to his synagogue, named the Society for the Advancement of Judaism, and in 1968 he opened a rabbinical school in Philadelphia.

Kaplan made two additional major contributions to Jewish life in America: the creation of a Jewish Community Center, where Jews could participate in a wide array of activities and programs, including arts, sports, swimming, and study; and the University of Judaism in Los Angeles, a professional school training Jewish educators and lay leaders.

The Orthodox Movement

Jewish immigrants arriving in America were forced to confront the question of their religious identity. Generally, Jews arriving from Eastern European countries tended to settle in close-knit communities where they built a synagogue and a school, and continued to observe their Jewish traditions. Established families in these communities would welcome newcomers and help them assimilate to American ways.

But finding a job was difficult, and many of the newcomers had to compromise their religious observance, such as working on Jewish holidays or the Sabbath. One such newcomer made the following notation in his diary: "Is this the celebrated freedom of America's soil, when in order to do business one must profane the holy Sabbath? O son of Israel, to follow God sincerely one must follow the holy Torah—but leading such a life none of us is able to observe the commandments."

American life proved to be a greater challenge to their religious observance than Jews could have anticipated. To make matters worse, by the mid-1800s Reform Judaism was taking hold in the United States, and, in the absence of resident rabbinical authorities, maintaining strict adherence to Jewish tradition became even more difficult.

Rabbi Isaac Lesser (1806–1868), an immigrant from Westphalia in Germany, took up the challenge of preserving traditional Judaism. Lesser traveled and lectured extensively as he campaigned to raise the awareness of American Jews about preserving their unique identity. He helped communities organize synagogues to strengthen their commitment to Judaism and a Jewish way of life.

Lesser advocated a return to Orthodox ways, believing that the Torah was given to the Jews by God on Mount Sinai, and that therefore, every word of the Torah is holy. Lesser taught that when the words of the Torah come into conflict with the everyday realities of American life, the realities must yield, not the Torah.

Despite his efforts, Lesser was not able not achieve his goal of unifying Orthodox rabbis under one central authoritative body. By 1888, there were approximately 120,000 Jewish families living on the Lower East Side of New York City, with only a few rabbis to serve the more than

100 small congregations. The Orthodox community had no leadership. Jewish education for butchers to slaughter meat in the kosher way, and religious functionaries to facilitate the important ceremonies of life, such as weddings, were inefficient at best, and certainly disorganized.

In 1888, Orthodox congregations in New York invited Rabbi Jacob Joseph (1842–1902) from Vilna in Russia to come to America and serve as their chief rabbi. Thousands showed up at the dock to welcome the distinguished rabbi. However, the decision to select Joseph was far from unanimous. He immediately instituted a minimum tax to be paid by members of the Orthodox community, which was met with widespread opposition. At the rabbi's first lecture at the synagogue Beth Hamidrash (The House of Study,) located at 54 Norfolk Street, he spoke softly in Yiddish and called on the congregants to conduct themselves with kindness and understanding, in the hope that his tenure would begin more smoothly. Unfortunately, this was not to be the case, and divisions within the community continued.

However, by 1902, hundreds of Orthodox rabbis united to form the Union of Orthodox Rabbis of the United States. Under Joseph's leadership, a yeshiva with uniquely American characteristics was created—a school where secular studies were combined with Jewish studies, leading students to become rabbis.

An institute of higher learning that would eventually be known as Yeshiva University opened its doors in 1897, on the Lower East Side of New York. The rabbinical school bore the name of Rabbi Isaac Elhanan (1817–1896), a great scholar. Leading the yeshiva was Dr. Bernard Revel (1885–1940), who presided over its growth and expansion. In 1945, the yeshiva officially became known as a university, and in 1955, Albert Einstein Medical School became part of Yeshiva University.

While today there are several different Orthodox groups, all Orthodox Jews share a dedication to the Torah. Orthodox Judaism sees itself as the direct continuation of the beliefs and practices that were handed down to Moses by God on Mount Sinai. In addition, Orthodox Jews believe all the Jewish laws are the direct word of God, and as such are binding and cannot be changed.

Hasidim in America

The Hebrew word *hasid* (*hasidim* is the plural) means "pious one." A movement known as Hasidism grew within Orthodox Judaism and

YESHIVA

An academy where young men study classical Jewish texts, including the Bible, Talmud, and codes of Jewish law, with the goal of becoming rabbis.

reached its highest level of success in the first half of the 1800s in Eastern Europe. At the beginning, Hasidic leaders were charismatic rabbis who attracted followers seeking a more spiritual, emotional way to worship as Jews. Their message was simple: worship God in joy. Their prayer reflected this philosophy, and was often combined with singing and dancing. The Hasidim called Jews to a spiritual renewal.

After World War II, virtually no Hasidic Jews remained in Europe. Those few who had survived the Holocaust immigrated to the United States, Israel, Canada, Australia, and Western Europe. Wherever they moved, they continued to live in small, family-based enclaves centered around a dynamic leader known as a rebbe, speaking Yiddish, and clinging to their ultra-Orthodox lifestyle.

Hasidim are easily recognized by their distinctive dress: men wear beards with sidelocks (called *pay'is*), black suits, coats, and hats. Hasidic women dress modestly in long dresses with high necklines and long sleeves. More than 60 different Hasidic groups are represented in Brooklyn, New York, most of which consist of only a few families. Among the different groups are Bobover (originally from Bobova, Poland), Belzer (from Belz, Poland), and Satmar (from Hungary). The largest groups of Hasidim are Lubavitch, also called Chabad, who send emissaries throughout the world to reach out to less observant Jews.

The Holocaust

Irrefutable historical evidence has proved that the Nazis put 6 million Jews to death from 1933 to 1945—2 million of them children. Beginning in 1933, when more than 500,000 Jews lived in Germany, the Nazi Party in Germany began its official policy of discrimination against the Jews. But the history of the party and its founder, Adolph Hitler, actually began 13 years earlier.

Hitler, with his persuasive personality and powerful organizational skills, dictated a policy of racist anti-Semitism to his new party. The mission adopted by the Nazi Party was to eradicate the less favorable races of society, specifically, Jews, Blacks, Slavs, and Roma (Gypsies). Hitler won control of the German Parliament, called the Reichstag, in a political campaign that appealed mostly to unemployed and lower-middle class voters, and by 1933, he was appointed chancellor of Germany.

Support for German Jews
At this rally in Philadelphia in the 1930s, thousands turned out to protest Hitler's treatment of Jews in Germany .

Nazi laws prohibited Jews from working for the government and other high-level positions, owning businesses, and attending universities. The turning point for Hitler's program to remove all Jews from Germany came on November 9, 1938—Kristallnacht, which means "Night of Broken Glass." On that night, more than 1,000 synagogues were burned, more than 7,000 Jewish businesses were destroyed, and hundreds of Jews were murdered.

After Kristallnacht, Jews who had been forced to live in ghettos were deported to concentration camps throughout Germany. These were camps based on forced labor and torture. Immediately after Kristallnacht, more than 30,000 Jews were sent to Dachau, Buchenwald, and Bergen-Belsen, where they experienced the worst possible living conditions.

By 1939, Hitler's armies had invaded and taken over the governments of Czechoslovakia, Austria, and Poland; Denmark, Norway, Holland, Belgium, and France joined the list in 1940. A final blow was dealt to Eastern European Jews in 1941 when Hitler invaded the Soviet Union, conquering Lithuania, Latvia, and the Ukraine, as well as Romania, Bulgaria, Yugoslavia, and Greece. Jews were forced to live in ghettos and were required to wear the Yellow Star of David inscribed with the word *Jude* (Jew) on their clothing. Food and medical supplies were in very short supply, and as a result, many Jews died of starvation and disease. Mobile killing squads made up of Nazi SS units and police called Einsatzgruppen murdered Soviet Jews.

Many obstacles faced the Jews who decided early on to leave Germany. In 1924, for example, the United States Congress passed the Johnson Immigration Act, which set quotas on the number of immigrants entering the United States from any single country. By 1939, the waiting period for entry was four to five years. France, Britain, Holland, and Belgium became waiting places for awhile, but by 1939 they had all closed their borders to Jewish immigrants from Germany.

Nazi persecution of the Jews reached its highest point between 1942 and 1945, when the Final Solution—a plan to murder all the Jews in Europe—was implemented in six concentration camps in Poland: Auschwitz-Birkenau, Belzec, Chelmno, Majdanek, Sobibor, and Treblinka. These camps, located in remote areas, were near railroad lines, so that the Jews could be delivered easily from any point in Europe. In the end, two-thirds of all the Jews in Europe were murdered. In some countries, the entire Jewish population was wiped out.

HOLOCAUST MEMORIAL MUSEUMS

In 1993, the United States Holocaust Memorial Museum, whose mission is to document the atrocities of the Nazis, opened its doors in Washington, D.C. You can learn more about the museum and the Holocaust by visiting www.ushmm.org. The Museum of Jewish Heritage in New York also chronicles the horrific experiences of the Holocaust and celebrates the survivors. Take a virtual tour at www.mjhnyc.org.

American Jews Respond

In 1933, after Adolph Hitler became chancellor of Germany, Rabbi Stephen S. Wise (1874–1949), then president of the World Jewish Congress, organized a protest at New York's Madison Square Garden. Joined by Jewish leaders in the United States and in England, Wise called on the American government to rescue Europe's Jews by bombing railroad lines leading to the concentration camps.

The Voyage of the St. Louis

On May 13, 1938, the St. Louis, a cruise ship, set sail from Hamburg, Germany, filled with Jews seeking to escape Nazi oppression. The Hamburg-America Line had sold visas to 907 Jews, at $150 to $300 per visa, that would allow them to sail to Cuba. In addition, agents charged the Jewish passengers another $150 each for landing certificates.

But neither the German government nor the officials of the Hamburg-America Line had any intention of allowing the Jews to disembark in Cuba. In a secret deal with the government of Cuba, the German government had invalidated the visas on May 5, and never told the passengers.

When the ship arrived at Havana Harbor, the Cubans refused to allow the Jewish refugees to disembark, and they sat on the ship for two weeks while the Cubans demanded that each Jewish family post a $500 bond to guarantee they would not end up as dependents of the Cuban government.

On June 1, 1939, the St. Louis was ordered to leave Havana Harbor, and it set sail on a return voyage to Germany. The story of the Jewish passengers on the St. Louis made headlines in major newspapers around the world. Pleas and telegrams to President Roosevelt went unanswered. The captain of the ship, showing compassion to the Jewish passengers, idled the ship past Florida while American Jewish leaders negotiated with Roosevelt, at one point offering to pay $500 for every Jewish passenger if the ship were allowed to dock in Miami. But permission was never granted.

Jews around the world pled with government leaders to allow the refugees to land at a new port. Finally, on June 17, 1939, an agreement was reached by Belgium, France, Britain, and Holland, to accept them. The St. Louis docked at Antwerp, Belgium, where the refugees were met by immigration officers who directed the families to locations in the four countries. They ended up in refugee camps, then concentration camps, and most of them died in the Holocaust.

Why didn't the United States allow the passengers on the St. Louis to land? The answer is anti-Semitism. The United States was still in an economic depression, and most Americans were too concerned with their own problems to even consider what was happening in Europe to the Jews. And anti-Semites in the United States, such as Father Couglin, a Catholic priest in Detroit, were blaming Jewish bankers and financiers for the Depression.

You can read more about the St. Louis in *Voyage of the Damned*, a book by Gordon Thomas and Max Morgan Witts.

In October 1943, 500 Orthodox rabbis participated in a march to the White House, where they requested a meeting with President Franklin D. Roosevelt. They sat silently, waiting for him, but Roosevelt refused to speak with them. Other Jewish leaders formed committees, protested, wrote letters, sent telegrams and did whatever they could to call attention to the genocide. But in the end, the Jewish community was unable to speak in one, unified voice, leaving its leaders powerless to make convincing arguments to the American public and, ultimately, to elected officials.

Not all Jewish voices were silenced. Laura Margolis (1904–1997) and her colleagues, for example, risked their lives as they supervised the distribution of millions of dollars in relief aid through the American Joint Distribution Committee. One of their most important projects was to help Jews stranded in Cuba reach a safe haven in Shanghai, China. Once in China, money provided food, clothing, and shelter for thousands of refugees.

Henry Morgenthau, Jr. (1856–1946), who served as United States Secretary of the Treasury, was another strong advocate for European Jews. Morgenthau's office obtained secret documents reporting the mass murder of Jews and passed them on to officials in the State Department. When no action was taken, Morgenthau took the information directly to President Roosevelt. Only then, did the President begin to initiate action on behalf of the Jews.

In May 1944, Morgenthau convinced the President to designate an old army base in Oswego, New York, for Jewish refugees. Ruth Gruber (b.1911), an employee of the Department of the Interior, was assigned to escort a group of refugees from Italy to the United States. Gruber, who spoke German fluently, learned firsthand what was happening to Jews in Europe and became an outspoken advocate for the welfare of these refugees.

When World War II ended, American soldiers were among those who liberated the concentration camps. Many of the Holocaust survivors came to the United States, but years passed before they were able to speak about their ordeal. Those who did speak painted a graphic picture of horror beyond all imagination. Nobel Prize winner Elie Wiesel was among the first to publish personal accounts.

"NEVER SHALL I FORGET"

Born in Sighet, Romania, in 1928, Elie Wiesel has dedicated his life to telling his story and the stories of millions of other Jews who went through the flames of the Holocaust. In 1944, at the age of 16, he, his family, and their entire community were sent to several concentration camps, including Auschwitz and Buchenwald. When he was liberated in 1945, he studied in Paris, then became a United States citizen in 1963. He has written more than 30 books about the Holocaust and has been awarded the Nobel Peace Prize and a Congressional Gold Medal of Achievement.

In his first book, *Night* (published in 1958), Wiesel wrote, "Never shall I forget that night, the first night in camp, which has turned my life into one long night, seven times cursed and seven times sealed. Never shall I forget that smoke. Never shall I forget the little faces of children, whose bodies I saw turned into wreaths of smoke beneath a silent blue sky. Never shall I forget those flames, which consumed my faith forever."

3

How Judaism Has Influenced American Culture

THROUGHOUT HISTORY, ARTISTS, MUSICIANS, AUTHORS, POETS, philosophers, scientists, athletes, and scholars have used their talents to enhance and enrich whatever society they find themselves in. Their work often combines their own personal vision with a reflection of the culture they live in and the things that bring meaning to their lives.

Jews throughout history have brought a special perspective to the cultures they have lived in. They have created great art, philosophy, and science that is influenced by both the country where they live and their almost 6,000 years of Jewish history.

It is no different in America. In virtually every area of American life and culture, Jewish people, both native and immigrant, have played a big part.

Yiddish Theater and the American Musical

Many expressions of Jewish culture grew from folk traditions that Eastern European immigrants brought with them, including dances, jokes, songs, legends, and superstitions. Anecdotal stories, told mainly in Yiddish, poked fun at the dismal conditions of their lives. What made these stories particularly Jewish was that in many cases they were based on a Biblical legend or proverb—only now the message was twisted and a completely new meaning emerged. The immigrants saw nothing wrong with poking some fun at the old ways, and even at themselves.

Yiddish theater had once thrived in Russia, and, beginning in the 1880s, it provided a unique artistic outlet for Eastern European immigrants living on the Lower East Side of New York. Yiddish, which combines elements of German, Polish, Russian, and Hebrew, was the mother tongue of these immigrants. It was spoken at home, at work in the sweatshops and factories, and in the synagogues. Adults learned about American life through Yiddish newspapers, such as *The Jewish Daily Forward* (see page 42), and the Yiddish theater.

But the theater offered immigrants more than just an opportunity to learn about America; it offered them an opportunity to laugh at themselves and at the situations they encountered as newly arrived "greenhorns." The audience, mostly families, enjoyed plays that reminded them of the old country, as well as melodramas that reminded them of the reasons they left. Historical stories, comedies, and tragedies provided an escape from their daily existence. In the Yiddish theater, Jewish characters were the heroes and heroines; they were flashy and noisy characters who sang, danced, and told jokes and wonderful stories.

The first Yiddish performance in New York took place in 1882. Abraham Goldfaden (1840–1908), a playwright from Russia, put together a troupe of actors to perform a play titled *The Sorceress*. The performance was a total fiasco. The musicians were late in arriving to the theater, the audience hissed and booed, and the show ended abruptly. Within a short time, however, other theatrical projects proved significantly more successful. Plays, including *Hamlet, Othello*, and a Jewish *King Lear*, proved popular, along with the absurd comedies and vaudeville.

How can we explain the explosion of talent from the Lower East Side of New York? One explanation is that in the early 1900s much of the theatrical business in New York was run by Jews. Jews opened booking agencies and ultimately joined forces to become major theatrical producers.

But it was more than just money or influence. Telling a funny story, impersonating an easily recognizable character, and belting out a catchy song drew audiences into theaters across the country, and it did not matter that the entertainer was Jewish. Talent is what mattered, not religious affiliation, or foreign accent, or country of origin. Jewish entertainers honed their talent on street corners, *bar mitzvah*

PRECEDING PAGE
Phone home
Steven Spielberg (shown here with E.T. star Drew Barrymore) is one of the world's most successful directors and producers. He has drawn on his Jewish heritage to create films that are both entertaining and thoughtful.

The Child Star

Molly Picon (1898–1992) stands out as an extraordinary actress, who, from a very young age, was able to transform Yiddish theater into an American phenomenon. Molly, the oldest daughter of Clara and Lewis Picon, was born on the Lower East Side on June 1, 1898. To earn extra money, Molly's mother, a costume seamstress, entered her in a variety of children's amateur night contests. At age five Molly made her theatrical debut—and won $5 for her first performance.

Moving to Philadelphia at a young age, Molly grew up on the stage. In 1919, when she married Jacob Kalich (1886–1975), manager of the Boston Grand Opera House, her mother sewed her wedding dress from the theater curtain. Together, Picon and Kalich wrote, produced, and acted in many successful Yiddish plays, including *Molly Dolly, Circus Girl*, and the most popular, *Schmendrick*, which told the story of a beloved nerd. Molly was so popular that in 1920, the Second Avenue Theater in New York was renamed the Molly Picon Theater. Molly and her husband joined the vaudeville circuit in the 1930s, where she began performing roles in English.

After World War II, Molly was among the first to entertain Jews housed in displaced persons camps (where refugees who no longer had a home were housed), bringing gifts for the women and children. Her performances combined Yiddish culture and American show business. As her career blossomed, she entered the newly developed moving picture industry, which eventually led her to play a variety of roles in radio and television. In 1964, Molly returned to New York to appear in the Broadway show *Milk and Honey*, and in 1971 she received an Oscar nomination for her role as Yenta the Matchmaker in the film version of *Fiddler on the Roof*.

and wedding celebrations, local dance halls, and cheap theaters. They borrowed material from a variety of sources: Irish, Jewish, African-American, vaudeville, and burlesque. Musical theater in New York, and eventually across America, was nourished by the talent and creativity that came out of Yiddish theater.

Musical comedy rose to its heights in the 20th century. A distinctly American art form, these shows included what is often referred to as "classic American music." The melodies and their lyrics have remained familiar long after the shows turned off their lights on Broadway.

Among the many creative Jewish people involved in the musical theater were Irving Berlin (1888–1989) and George Gershwin (1898–1937). Berlin wrote a large number of hit songs that sold millions of records and were heard on stage and in movies. Ironically, one of the best-selling records of all time—"White Christmas"—was written by this Jewish composer. Berlin, a Russian immigrant, also wrote "God Bless America" to show his deep love for his adopted homeland.

George Gershwin wrote music for a variety of successful shows, including *Strike Up the Band* and *Funny Face*. But he may be best remembered for his important compositions that bridged the gap between traditional classical music and that uniquely American art form—jazz. His jazz symphonies *Rhapsody in Blue* and *An American in Paris* still inspire musicians and composers today.

The Borscht Belt and American Comedy

At about the same time as Yiddish theater was growing in popularity on the Lower East Side, another genre of entertainment was taking shape. In the late 1800s, Jews who were wealthy enough to take a nice vacation were often shut out of hotels, resorts, and clubs. Judge Henry Hilton, owner of the prestigious Grand Union Hotel in Saratoga Springs, New York, announced: "Israelites are not welcome." Other resort locations, including Cape May and Long Branch in New Jersey, followed Hilton's lead. Newspapers carried these announcements, often accompanied by insulting caricatures of Jews.

As a result of this exclusionary policy, wealthy German Jews built luxurious hotels, resorts, and clubs for themselves. And, after the mass immigration of the 1880s, Eastern European Jews did the same, building lower-priced hotels for themselves. To escape New York's hot, humid summers, Jews headed for the Catskill Mountains, to towns including Ellenville, Monticello, and Kiamisha Lake. These resorts came to be known as the "Borscht Belt," after a Russian beet soup that was often served in their dining rooms.

Jewish entertainers, including Milton Berle, George Burns, Henny Youngman, Red Buttons, Jerry Lewis, Eddie Cantor, Mel Brooks, and many others, would travel a circuit through these towns performing humorous shows, usually with music. Like their colleagues who performed in the theater, these actors eventually moved west, where the entertainment industry was developing—in many cases to Las Vegas, where they became headliners at the casino hotels.

Many popular Jewish entertainers faced anti-Semitism as they tried to become famous outside the world of the Borscht Belt. As a result, some opted to change their names to something that sounded "less Jewish": Stern became Shaw, Kessler became Kirkland.

It is interesting to note that after World War II, as television became widespread, popular shows included *The Goldbergs* and the *Texaco Star Theater* starring Milton Berle—whose real name was Mendel

VAUDEVILLE

A type of theatrical entertainment that had its origins in minstrel shows, concert saloons, and beer gardens. Vaudeville performances featured a variety of acts: musical numbers, magicians, dancers, jugglers, and comic routines. This type of live variety entertainment was popular until moving pictures were introduced.

BURLESQUE

This type of theatrical entertainment was popular from the 1870s and featured parodies of popular theatrical, literary, and musical works. A typical burlesque show contained songs and dances performed by women and comedy routines performed by men. The "strip tease" became the most popular ingredient of burlesque.

Berlinger. Berle, who died in 2002, is credited with paving the way for Jews in popular entertainment. He used English and Yiddish together to tell his stories and jokes. Because of Berle's success, the use of Yiddish words and expressions became commonplace among comedians.

In 1965, Wallace Markfield wrote about the influence of Jewish comedians: "Turn to any TV variety show, await the stand-up comic, and chances are good that he'll come on with accents and gestures and usages whose origins are directly traceable to the Borscht Belt by way of the East European shtetl [small town or village] and the corner candy store. We are getting, on TV situation comedies, Indians behaving like members of the Shmohawk tribe, abstract painters named Schmeer, Chinese valets mixing batters of kreplach [a dumpling for soup], Russian spies pausing for 'a nice glass tea.'" (Markfield's comments are quoted in *World of Our Fathers* by Irving Howe, published in 1976.)

By the 1970s, actor, comedian, and producer Mel Brooks was using this vocabulary extensively in his movies, including *Blazing Saddles*, where an Indian chief begins a speech in Yiddish, and *Frisco Kid*, where

It Takes Chutzpah to Be a Mensch

Here are some Yiddish words that have come into common English use:

chutzpah: a big helping of nerve; super-confidence

ersatz: an inferior substitute; a fake

gelt: money

kibitz: to gossip or meddle

klutz: a clumsy person

kvetch: a complainer; to complain

maven: a connoisseur

megillah: a long story

mensch: one who possesses the qualities of a gentleman; an honest, honorable person

meshungina: a little crazy

nebbish: a little nerd

nosh: to eat a little something; snack

oy vey: generally expressing a negative emotion

plotz: burst

schlep: to drag or carry something heavy

schmate: a rag, or another name for everyday clothing

schmeer: something you spread on a bagel, such as cream cheese; to spread all over

schmaltz: something that plays on the emotions (the word literally means rendered chicken fat)

schmutz: dirt

shtick: an act or routine; a way of behaving

tuchis or tush: the backside

actor Gene Wilder screams "oy gevalt" as his horse rides off without him. Brooks' stereotypical Jewish characters, Bialystock and Blum, played by Nathan Lane and Matthew Broderick, recently won more than a dozen Tony Awards for their roles as dishonest Broadway producers in the smash Broadway show *The Producers*.

The Movies

The entertainment industry was not limited to New York. In 1912 a revolutionary change came to American entertainment with the birth of a new industry—motion pictures—in Hollywood, California. Pioneers included Jesse Lasky and Samuel Goldwyn (both Jewish), who hired their friend Cecil B. De Mille to direct their first feature film, and the Warner brothers (also Jewish), who cast Jewish vaudeville actor Al Jolson in their first movie that included sound, *The Jazz Singer*.

Since those early years, numerous Jewish actors and actresses, directors, and producers have worked in the motion picture industry both in front of and behind the camera. The Marx Brothers, Edward G. Robinson, Joel Grey, Walter Matthau, Dustin Hoffman, and Barbra Streisand were just a few of those in front of the camera, and Louis B. Mayer and Steven Spielberg were among the people behind it.

Four funny guys
The Marx Brothers (from left, Chico, Zeppo, Groucho, and Harpo) successfully made the transition from vaudeville to the movies with such classics as A Night at the Opera *and* Monkey Business.

In the case of Steven Spielberg, the movies *E.T.* and *Schindler's List* were not only box-office hits, but also changed people's perceptions of the world. *E.T.* showed us how a true outsider can find a place among open-minded people. *Schindler's List* poignantly documented the heroism of a single person who managed to save hundreds of lives during the Holocaust. For both these films, Spielberg drew upon his experiences and heritage as a Jew.

A more recent phenomenon is the growing number of Jewish Film Festivals that offer opportunities for a wider range of people to learn about Jews and the Jewish community. Last year, Jewish Film Festivals were held in Washington, D.C., New York, San Diego, Palm Beach, Miami, Seattle, San Francisco, and more than 30 other communities across the United States.

Television

David Sarnoff's (1891–1971) first job in America was as a telegraph messenger. (In the days before radio, telegraphs were used to send messages between cities. These messages would then be printed out and hand-delivered by messengers.) He later became a wireless radio operator in New York. An ambitious inventor, playing with "the radio music box," Sarnoff set the stage for the opening of the Radio Corporation of America (RCA) and later created the National Broadcasting Company's (NBC) first radio network.

Sarnoff was among the first to recognize the potential of radio, and later television, to bring Americans together in a way that would transform our culture. In 1946, he introduced the first television set to the American public. While Sarnoff was not the actual inventor of television (that was Philo Farnsworth and others), he was among those most responsible for making it popular. NBC became one of the first television networks. Soon the new invention was in nearly every American home. Its impact on both America and the world is incredible, and many point to Sarnoff as the man who first understood its incredible potential.

Classical Music

Great music transcends time, nationality, and ethnic identity. Jewish musicians, including pianist Arthur Rubinstein, violinists Jasha Heifetz and Isaac Stern, clarinetist and bandleader Benny Goodman, composer and conductor Leonard Bernstein, and opera singers Richard Tucker

JERRY SEINFELD

Jerry Seinfeld was born and raised in New York City and graduated from Queens College after majoring in theater and communications. He was already a successful stand-up comic when he co-created the hugely popular television sitcom *Seinfeld* in 1990. In the show, Jerry played himself, a single comic living in New York, who has to cope with all the trivial annoyances of life. For his work on the number-one-rated show, Seinfeld won several Emmys, Golden Globes, and Screen Actors Guild Awards. His comedy, while rooted in the everyday life of four New Yorkers, also continued the long tradition of popular Jewish-American comedians.

and Jan Peerce, have appeared regularly in the great concert halls and theaters around the world. Bernstein also composed the music for *West Side Story*, a modern retelling of Shakespeare's *Romeo and Juliet*. And Robert Merrill is known just as well for his opera singing as he is for singing the national anthem at Yankee Stadium in New York. What was so special about these musicians? They were all Americans.

Art

Perhaps because so many Jews were recent immigrants from Europe, where art was being rapidly transformed at the turn of the 20th century, or perhaps because Jews understood what it feels like to be outside of the predominant cultural trends, Jewish artists and gallery owners played a visionary role in bringing modern art to the United States.

Max Weber (1881–1961) was among the first artists to carry the modernist revolution to the United States. He was born in the western Russian (now Polish) town of Bialystok, a center for textile production. Weber once said that his earliest memory was of his grandfather mixing colorful fabric dyes, which instilled in him a love of bold colors and forms. When he was 10, Weber's family emigrated to Brooklyn, New York, and seven years later he entered Pratt Institute in Brooklyn.

In 1905 Weber went to Paris, where he studied with Henri Matisse and witnessed the development of many radical new artistic styles. Upon returning to America in 1909, he forged a personal vision from these many styles, adding elements of the art of Aztec, Mayan, Egyptian, Greek, Oceanic, and northern Pacific cultures. Weber became one of the first American artists to apply these diverse approaches to printmaking, frequently using color at a time when most other American artists made only black-and-white prints.

With the death of his father in 1917, Weber turned to his spiritual and cultural Jewish heritage, and became one of the few American modern artists to adopt religious subjects for his work.

Photographer and gallery owner Alfred Stieglitz (1864–1946) has been called one of the most significant influences in American cultural life in the period before World War II. He was among the first to introduce modern European art to the American public, organizing the first exhibitions in the United States of work by Pablo Picasso, Henri Matisse, Georges Braque, and Paul Cézanne, among others. He was also one of the first to support American modernist artists such as Geor-

One of the most important Jewish contributions to American culture can be seen on tables at home and in restaurants. Is there anyone in America who has not eaten a bagel? Many popular foods in America have Jewish roots. Here is a partial list.

bagel (often served with a *schmeer* of cream cheese)

blintz (sort of like manicotti, stuffed with sweet cheese or fruit)

chicken soup (sometimes called "Jewish penicillin")

chopped liver

deli meats, such as **brisket**, **corned beef**, and **pastrami**

gefilte fish (cakes made of cooked, chopped fish)

knish (a sort of potato burrito)

kreplach (little stuffed dumplings)

latkes (potato pancakes)

lox (smoked salmon)

matzah balls (balls of matzah dough usually served in chicken soup)

American Jewish writers are among those who took advantage of the opportunities that awaited them in the United States. In many cases, these American writers mixed Yiddish and Eastern European cultural influences into their works. Their writing contains material gathered from traditional Jewish texts, as well as influences from their countries of origin. This is not to imply, however, that Jewish writers only used Jewish themes or sources in their work. Quite the contrary, works written by Jewish authors cover a wide variety of subject matter and themes. Their energy, creativity, and achievement points to their successful assimilation into American culture.

Since World War II, American Jewish writers have become part of the mainstream in American literature. Jews and non-Jews enjoy their books, plays, essays, and articles. Among the most well-known Jewish American authors are Philip Roth, Erica Jong, Arthur Miller, Norman Mailer, Leon Uris, Irving Stone, and Chaim Potok. In 1976, author Saul Bellow won the Nobel Prize for Literature.

The prestigious Pulitzer Prize for literature has been awarded to several Jewish writers. Philip Roth is known for his satirical portraits

The Business of Publishing

en described as "The People of the Book," Jewish nors and publishers have enjoyed successful ca- s throughout history both in Europe and the Unit- States. Major American publishing companies cre- d or owned by Jews, including Alfred A. Knopf; on & Schuster; and Farrar, Straus, Giroux; have in- duced American readers to works written by great erican authors such as Robert Penn Warren, Joseph rad, John Steinbeck, and Ernest Hemingway.

Specializing in Hebrew and Yiddish language ks is the Block Publishing Company, the oldest ish-owned publishing company in America, begun 854. The Jewish Publication Society, founded in ladelphia in 1888, continues to operate today.

In the late 19th century, Jews entered the newspaper and periodical business. In 1986, Adolph Ochs, from Chattanooga, Tennessee, acquired *The New York Times* when it was on the brink of bankruptcy and built it into one of America's most influential newspapers.

Ernest Gruening, who served as governor of and senator from Alaska, was also a newspaperman. When not employed as a politician, he served as editor of *The Nation* and *The New York Tribune*.

Walter Lippmann's columns in *The New York Herald Tribune* played an influential role in foreign affairs. Following in his footsteps are columns written in *The New York Times* by William Safire.

gia O'Keeffe, Arthur Dove, John Marin, Marsden Hartley, and Charles Demuth.

Stieglitz was also among the first artists to understand the great potential of photography as an art form, and his photographs of immigrants arriving at Ellis Island in New York are among his most poignant. Stieglitz, however, was not an immigrant himself; he was born in Hoboken, New Jersey.

Another photographer who has transformed the way we look at things is Richard Avedon (b.1923). Avedon was born in New York City and trained as a photographer in the United States Merchant Marine in World War II. His elegant, innovative fashion photography appeared first in *Harper's Bazaar* and then in *Vogue*. In contrast to this work, Avedon's sharply focused, bluntly realistic photos of presidents, writers, celebrities, and everyday people seems to penetrate beyond their faces and present portraits of their personalities.

Peggy Guggenheim (1898–1979), like Stieglitz, helped transform the way Americans think about art by bringing exciting new artists and art movements to public attention. She was the daughter of Benjamin Guggenheim and Florette Seligman, and grew up in New York City, where her father played a leading role in the investment banking industry. When Peggy was in her 20s, she worked as a volunteer in a bookshop, Sunwise Turn, where she met and became friendly with authors, artists, and other intellectuals. In 1938, she opened her first art gallery in London. This was the beginning of a long career that she dedicated to collecting contemporary art.

In 1942, she opened her museum and gallery, Art of This Century, in New York, which became a top venue for exhibiting works of contemporary art. She introduced a number of important American artists to the world, including Jackson Pollock. In 1969, she was invited to show her extensive collection of art at the Solomon R. Guggenheim Museum in New York City. At the end of this exhibition, she decided to donate her entire collection to the Solomon R. Guggenheim Foundation.

Literature

Jewish families have gained a reputation for emphasizing the importance of education for their children. Jewish immigrants always insisted on sending their children (or at least the boys) to school. Often, the children spoke English before their parents did.

ART IMIT
Edna Ferbe
was a nove
Among her
works are S
Giant. In bo
Ferber drew
perience of

Ferber g
coal-mining
where she f
anti-Semitisr
oirs, she wro
wasn't a ben
cause it was
ish citizens. I
Jewish citizer
a benighted t
was bad, the
its people we
resentful, and
was, for a pla
locality, an un
rough elemen
as could be, th
for a minority
vent their diss:
the world. And
were, and ther
scapegoat of th
though I had a
it in Ottumwa,
of it in New Yor
that these Ottu
were more enri
valuable than al
luxury of the Ne

of middle-class American Jews, and Arthur Miller for his realistic dramas, including *Death of a Salesman* and *A View From the Bridge*. Norman Mailer, a novelist and essayist, uses his talents to write about a wide variety of contemporary topics. He was awarded a Pulitzer Prize for *Armies in the Night*, a first-hand description of a demonstration that took place in front of the Pentagon in 1969 to protest the Vietnam War.

Most recently, *Tuesdays with Morrie*, a book about the relationship of a teacher and student, written by Mitch Album, was on *The New York Times* bestseller list for more than two years. *The Red Tent*, a contemporary novel based on the Biblical story of Dinah, written by Anita Diament, captured the imagination of thousands of women. It, too, was on the bestseller list for more than a year.

The Sporting Life

The American sports of basketball and baseball were very popular with Jewish athletes. Beginning in 1918, the South Philadelphia Hebrew Association sponsored basketball teams made up entirely of Jewish players. The Hebrews, a basketball team from South Philadelphia, practiced at the Young Men's Hebrew Association (YMHA). After World War II, Eddie Gottlieb, a former player for The Hebrews, organized the Philadelphia Warriors—the team that won the very first National Basketball Association (NBA) championship in 1946. Basketball also drew Jewish players on college campuses, including Temple University in Philadelphia and City College in New York.

On the baseball field, players such as Hank Greenberg, Sandy Koufax, and Shawn Green stand as examples to all Jewish kids who dream of playing professional baseball. Despite missing four seasons at the prime of his career to fight in World War II, and sitting out another season with a broken wrist, Hank Greenberg still hit 331 home runs, including 40 or more in six seasons. He was voted the Most Valuable Player in 1935 and 1940. On the last day of the 1945 season, Greenberg's ninth-inning grand slam won the Pennant for the Detroit Tigers.

In 1984, Harold and Meir Ribalow wrote the book *Jewish Baseball Stars*, which includes the story of Al Rosen. According to the father-and-son authors, "Al Rosen, the tough and talented third baseman of the Cleveland Indians, would stand up to anyone who dared to insult his ancestry. In 1953, he was voted the American League Most Valuable Player, in an unprecedented unanimous vote." At that time, "Rosen

JEWISH OLYMPIANS
Six Jewish Americans participated in the 2002 Winter Olympic Games in Salt Lake City: four figure skaters, one speed skater, and one hockey player. Sarah Hughes brought home the gold medal for figure skating. Her American teammates included Sasha Cohen, Amber Corwin, Sarah Abitol, Dan Weinstein, and Sara DeCosta. Past Jewish Olympic medalists include swimmers Mark Spitz, Lenny Krayzelburg, and Jason Lezak, gymnast Kerri Strug, and speed skater Dan Weinstein.

declared that he would be willing to change his name to Rosenthal or Rosenstein to become even more apparently Jewish." After retiring, Rosen said, "I wanted it to be, 'Here comes one Jewish kid that every Jew in the world can be proud of.'"

Sports writers still argue about whether Sandy Koufax, a left-handed pitcher for the Los Angeles Dodgers, was the greatest pitcher ever to play the game. He won 25 games in a season three times, had five straight ERA titles, and threw 382 strikeouts in 1965. His blazing fastball and devastating curveball enabled him to pitch no-hitters in four consecutive seasons, with a perfect game in 1965.

Moe Berg, a catcher for the Tigers, also spied for the Allies during World War II. Ron Blomberg of the New York Yankees was the first designated hitter in the Major Leagues in 1973. Ken Holtzman, a pitcher for the Los Angeles Dodgers, threw two no-hitters.

Shawn Green came from a secular family, and knew little about his Jewish heritage. A top student, Green attended Stanford University but left without graduating to pursue his baseball career. As Jewish communities welcomed Green, he realized that he was becoming a role model for Jewish children. Green, formerly an outfielder with the Toronto Blue Jays, was traded in 2001 to the Los Angeles Dodgers. Since returning to Los Angeles, Green has begun to play a greater role in raising awareness for Jewish charitable organizations. Like Greenberg and Koufax, Green also refused to play baseball on Yom Kippur in 2001.

In addition to players, a significant number of Jews have entered the field of sports journalism and broadcasting. Among the nationally recognized broadcasters are Marv Albert (NBC), Al Bernstein, Linda Cohn, Rich Eisen, Hank Goldberg, and Jeremy Schapp (ESPN), Bonnie Bernstein (CBS), Larry Merchant (HBO), Suzy Shuster (Fox Sports Net), and Mel Allen, who was best known as the voice of the New York Yankees. The voice of Howard Cosell will forever be connected with Monday Night Football and the boxer Mohammed Ali. And runner Marty Glickman was removed from the American team in the 1936 Berlin Olympics to avoid offending Hitler, but gained fame as a broadcaster for the New York Jets.

Science and Technology

Immigrant Jewish parents recognized that education was the key for their children, and while many left the classroom in search of adventure

---

SOME THINGS ARE MORE IMPORTANT

Playing for the Detroit Tigers, Hank Greenberg made history in 1934 when he refused to play in a playoff game on Yom Kippur. Although the Tigers lost that game, they went on to win the Pennant, and Greenberg went on to win the respect of the entire city of Detroit.

Sandy Koufax also refused to play on Yom Kippur—October 6, 1965, the first game of the World Series—and went to synagogue instead. Koufax pitched the seventh game in the Series against the Twins, and won.

Both Greenberg and Koufax were inducted into the National Baseball Hall of Fame in Cooperstown, New York.

Simply the best
Sandy Koufax pitched no-hitters in four consecutive seasons—a feat that has never been equalled.

on the streets, those who remained managed to graduate and enter professional careers. Sociologists have shown that the American public school system in the period after World War II was the single most influential factor that produced so many Jewish doctors, lawyers, scientists, writers, and other professionals.

Writer and comedian Harry Golden once described his childhood in the 1900s. "Education was the key to everything. You walked up to your flat in a tenement house and from behind every second door would come shouting and the arguments over the issues of the day. Meanwhile, the kids emptied out the local branch of the public library. Even the old folks were concerned with education. There were night schools, day schools, before-going-to-work schools, private schools, business schools, schools for learning English, and classes in civics."

When major universities imposed quotas to limit the number of Jewish applicants, the number of students at more open institutions of higher learning, such as City College in New York City and Temple University in Philadelphia, soared, and many of those Jewish students

The genius
Albert Einstein is one of the most influential thinkers of the 20th century. His theories on the structure and origins of the universe continue to be proven true.

went on to make significant contributions to American society. In more recent years, large numbers of Jewish students have consistently gained entry to Ivy League universities.

A disproportionate number of Jewish scientists have been awarded the Nobel Prize. Since 1908, 43 Jewish scientists in the field of biomedical studies alone have received this prestigious award, 21 of them Americans. Eleven Nobel Prizes have been awarded to Jewish economists, and Jews have excelled in other fields, as well.

Joseph Goldberger was a Jewish doctor who pioneered preventive medicine. Working for the U.S. Public Health Service, he studied yellow fever and typhus in Cuba and Mexico to learn more about how they are transmitted and how the cycle of contagion can be broken.

Drs. Jonas Salk and Albert Sabin discovered and developed two polio vaccines that have virtually eliminated the disease.

Physicist Robert Oppenheimer served as director of the Los Alamos laboratory, where the first atomic bomb was developed. After World War II, Oppenheimer served as chairman of the General Advisory Council of the Atomic Energy Commission.

Albert Michelson set the stage for some of Albert Einstein's most important work when he measured the exact speed of light. And Albert Einstein, a giant among scientists, introduced the world to the theory of relativity and described the nature of the universe. Einstein became an American citizen along with other German scientists who fled the Nazis.

When it comes to exploring the nature of space, Einstein is not the only Jewish American who has taken up the challenge. Astronauts Judith Resnick, Jeffrey Hoffman, Martin Fettman, Scott Horowitz, Ellen Shulman Baker, John Grunsfeld, Marsha Ivins, and David Wolf share this distinction with pride. Dr. Martin Fettman was the first veterinarian in space. Scott Horowitz served as the pilot of the Atlantis shuttle in May 2000. A colonel in the Air Force, Horowitz was a fighter pilot before entering the NASA program. Astronaut Marsha Ivins' NASA biography points out that she has flown a record 1,400 hours in space.

Business and Industry

At the beginning of the 20th century, many major American corporations limited the number of Jewish employees they were willing to hire. Still, Jewish businessmen were able to rise to the very top levels in publicly owned companies. For example, Gerard Swope served as president of General Electric from 1922 to 1940, and Irving Shapiro was the chairman of the DuPont Company from 1973 to 1981. While Swope played down his Jewish identity, Shapiro emphasized his. After working as a lawyer for the Justice Department, Shapiro rejected advice to change his last name in order to increase his career opportunities in the corporate world.

Andrew Grove, a Holocaust survivor, combined his business, technology, and entrepreneurial skills to create the largest microchip company in the world. The Intel Corporation has enabled the computer industry to provide data processing capability at eye-popping speed.

4

Jewish Impact on American Social Issues

BOTH BIBLICAL AND RABBINIC WRITINGS ILLUSTRATE JUDAISM'S concern with social issues. There are four Jewish concepts which, taken together, provide a solid understanding of the Jewish ideas of charity and social concern. In Hebrew, these are called *tzedakah, gemilut chasadim, ohr l'goyim*, and *tikkun olam*. Let's take a look at what each means, and how they relate to American Jewish life.

Tzedakah. *Tzedakah* is often defined as "charity," but its Hebrew root word means "righteousness or justice." In Deuteronomy (a book of the Bible) we find the following instruction: "*Tzedek, tzedek* you shall pursue" or "Justice, justice you shall pursue." This commandment to pursue justice has been interpreted as a commandment to act in ways that make the world a fair place, or to do *tzedakah*. Thus, *tzedakah* is not selfless giving, but commanded righteousness. In other words, it is the duty of every Jewish person to give, both of time and worldly goods.

Gemilut Chasadim. *Gemilut chasadim* literally means "love, grace, compassion, and kind deeds." Although the concept of *tzedakah* does not imply altruistic giving, *gemilut chasadim* does. *Gemilut chasadim* are acts of loving kindness, such as burying the dead, visiting the sick, providing interest-free loans, doing chores for the old or the frail, or helping the poor.

The Jewish people are commanded to give *tzedaka*h and encouraged to do *gemilut chasadim* by the Bible, where specific examples are pointed out as models of the right way to live.

Ohr l'Goyim. The ancient Israelites were also inspired by the prophet Isaiah to bring their own sense of justice, righteousness, and ethical monotheism to the world. In the Bible book Isaiah 49:6, God says, "I will also make you a light of nations, That My salvation may reach the ends of the earth." The idea that the Jewish people are commanded to be a light of nations, *ohr l'goyim*, has inspired the American Jewish community to aid not only other Jews, but other communities in need, as well. Organizations supported and organized by Jews often provide programs that help entire communities, not just Jews.

Tikkun Olam. *Tikkun olam* means "building a better world," and instructs Jews to improve the world by encouraging people to act ethically and to help others. Jews today use the term *tikkun olam* to describe the activities of people who strive to improve the world by volunteering, whether it is for a soup kitchen or a political rally. Many Jews donate money or their time to help individuals improve their standard of living and to provide food, clothing, and shelter to those in need.

These four concepts have motivated the American Jewish community to come together and provide for their own needs as well as for the needs of the non-Jewish community. The Jewish concepts of *tzedakah* and *gemilut chasadim* motivate Jews to give charity and volunteer to help the needy. The idea of *tikkun olam* encourages the Jewish people to do these things in order to build a better world. Finally, the Jewish mandate to be a light of nations, *ohr l'goyim*, inspires the Jewish community to provide aid to non-Jews as well as Jews. Thus, Judaism and Jewish communal programs have long supported the pluralistic nature of American culture. In this chapter, we will learn about the concrete programs and activities that these ideas inspired in the American Jewish community.

Social Welfare: 1654–1820

Jews from Spain and Portugal, or *sephardim*, were the first Jews to arrive in North America. These people came by way of the West Indies, South America, or directly from Europe. After 1600, their *ashkenazi*

Tikkun Olam

The concept of *tikkun olam*, which literally means "building a better world," originated in Jewish mysticism. Isaac Luria (1534–1572) was a Jewish mystic. The facts about his life are shrouded in mystery and legend. What is known for sure is that he grew up in Egypt, where he studied classical Jewish texts with scholars of the time. Some time later, while conducting business, he moved to Safed, a small town in northern Israel that was a center for the Jewish mystical movement, known as Kabbalah. There, he began his study of texts written in the mystic tradition.

In his writings, Luria outlined three stages of Jewish experience: 1) God creates the world, history begins, and then God withdraws. 2) Everything that was created is shattered, like a pottery jar, and the pieces (shards) are scattered throughout the world. 3) There is a period of restoration (*tikkun olam*), during which people perform acts that put the pieces of creation back together again to create a new reality.

Luria explained that each time a Jew performs one of the 613 commandments found in the Torah, he or she is picking up the shattered shards of God's creation and restoring God's light in the world.

Today, American Jews often use the concept of *tikkun olam* to describe their volunteer efforts to solve social problems. *Tikkun olam* has become a phrase that means building a better world for all people, inspiring programs such as mentoring programs, food pantries, nursing home visits, and after-school activities for disadvantaged children. Through this kind of social action, American Jews bring God's light back into the world.

cousins, Jews from northern and eastern Europe, joined them.

Early Jewish communities centered on the synagogue. The synagogue itself was a resource for Sabbath and festival observances, burial rites, marriage ceremonies, and providing kosher food. These synagogue communities gave money to the poor, who were often widows, in the form of yearly allowances, clothing, and medical care, and offered shelter for traveling Jews. In the 18th century, for example, New York's Shearith Israel synagogue spent 10 percent of its income on Jewish social needs.

Providing for the needs of any community requires leadership and money. There were requirements upon members of congregations to attend religious services, to follow Jewish law, and to serve in leadership positions in the synagogue. These leaders worked hard to raise money and to provide services to those in need.

In any community, burying the dead is an important activity. There are specific Jewish rituals that accompany burials which only other Jews can provide. Many early American Jewish families could not afford to bury their loved ones properly, so the community paid for the funerals.

Visiting the sick was also an important communal activity motivated by the Jewish concept of *gemilut chasadim*. When people were sick, they often could not leave their houses, so community members would visit them, bringing food, helping with the household chores, and providing comfort.

Finally, there were many poor Jews in America's early years. Jewish concepts such as *gemilut chasadim* inspired Jewish Americans to give loans to other Jews without charging them interest. In addition to providing loans, the Jewish community also helped poor Jews get the food, clothing, and housing they needed to live.

The first migration of Jews to the United States was not very large. Before 1820, only a few thousand Jews lived in the New World. Because of their small numbers, these Jewish communities were able to provide relief to just about every individual who needed it.

Social Welfare: 1820–1880

The experience of the German-Jewish American community differed dramatically from the story of the early Jewish settlers. Instead of focusing on the synagogue as community centers, the German Jews chose to establish meeting houses much like those of non-Jews. These meeting houses provided a sense of community without demanding the same adherence to Jewish law as the synagogues. Membership in the lodge called B'nai B'rith, founded in 1843, reflected the Jewish experience with the European Kehillah (see the box on page 78). Synagogues still flourished, but they were not the centers of Jewish communal life.

Instead, charitable organizations, such as the Hebrew Benevolent Society, took care of many of the social welfare responsibilities of American Jewish communities. Some of these benevolent societies were connected to a synagogue, but many were not. The activities of these benevolent societies included *gemilut chasadim*, acts of loving kindness, such as visiting the sick.

Not only did these social welfare activities provide relief for those in need, but they also provided opportunities for communal leadership. It was considered an honor to be involved in the rituals surrounding burial and to contribute to interest-free loans and money for the poor.

Examples of benevolent societies included the United Hebrew Benevolent Association in New York (founded in 1822), the Female Hebrew Benevolent Society in Philadelphia (1819), the Association for the Relief of Jewish Widows and Orphans in New Orleans (1860), and the Jewish Foster Home of Philadelphia (1855).

The American Jewish community also organized Jewish orphanages and Jewish hospitals, such as Mt. Sinai Hospital in New York. By 1860, the settled German-Jewish American community had already formed many societies, associations, and organizations to fulfill the four social obligations of the Jewish community. However, the German-Jewish American community had not yet experienced their greatest challenge in providing social welfare to their people.

The Great Wave of Immigrants

Before 1880, a quarter of a million Jews lived in the United States. Between 1880 and 1920, more than 2 million Jews immigrated to this country, most of them from Eastern Europe. Unlike their German Jewish counterparts, who had come from educated, urban families, these new immigrants were from poor rural villages and had little education.

This massive wave of immigration resulted in the resettlement of eight times as many Jews as were already living in the United States. Millions of poor Jewish immigrants arriving in America within 40 years created problems unforeseen in American Jewish history.

Most of the settled Jews in America in 1880 were from central Europe or Germany. They began to arrive in the 1820s and spent the following 60 years establishing their place in American society. Although they still maintained their identity as Jews, they had largely adopted the American way of life.

But the Eastern European immigrants maintained the clothing and customs of their Eastern European villages. The Eastern European Jews' traditional practices and Old World customs clashed with the German Jews' already Americanized customs and values.

Children of the covenant
This photograph was taken during a 1932 meeting of the B'nai B'rith organization. The name means "children of the covenant." Today B'nai B'rith has a number of projects to support Jews worldwide, from education to financial support to tracking down former Nazis and bringing them to justice.

A Communal Tradition

Historically, the Jewish people have been defined by their group consciousness—their belief that they are all descended from Abraham and his children, or at least that they are descended from people who recognize this heritage. They also believe in the authority of Jewish law, as expressed in the Torah.

In medieval and early modern Europe, Jews often found themselves living in autonomous political and economic communities. An autonomous community is one in which the people of the community establish and follow their own laws while living within the borders of a nation. These Jewish communities in Europe were responsible for their own economic and political lives. The European organized Jewish community was called the Kehillah.

The leaders of the Kehillah in Europe used Jewish law to determine the laws of their own community. These European Jewish community leaders collected taxes, established courts to maintain order, negotiated with government authorities, and organized welfare agencies. Thus, when millions of Jewish immigrants arrived in the United States at the dawn of the 20th century, they brought with them the idea of communal responsibility; that people who share a common heritage are responsible for one another. This idea of community provided a model for established American Jews to take care of the needs of the American Jewish community as a whole.

In fact, the German Jews were somewhat embarrassed by the customs and appearance of the Eastern European Jews. As the settled Jewish community worked to alleviate the poverty of many of the new immigrants, they also used relief programs to accelerate the integration of these immigrants into American society. This process was called Americanization. The process included teaching the immigrants to speak English, helping them to find jobs, and introducing them to American leisure activities. One program used the Boy Scouts of America to help the immigrant children fit in better, because it provided boys with exercise and taught the American values of individualism and self-reliance.

The most pressing problem of the Jewish immigrants was their appalling living conditions. The housing tenements on the Lower East Side of New York City at the dawn of the 20th century had little light and no fresh air. Often people dumped their sewage into the street from their windows. In addition, the work places, often referred to as sweatshops, had no ventilation and were serious fire hazards.

Early Jewish social welfare programs focused on decreasing poverty and providing the Jewish immigrants with services specific to Judaism. These included burial societies that used the proper Jewish burial rituals and employment agencies that understood that many Jews would not work on Saturdays, the Jewish Sabbath.

The Jewish Federation Idea

By 1860, New York contained 44 Jewish charitable and benevolent groups, mostly established by German-American Jews. Each of these early groups in the American Jewish community focused on one particular goal, such as providing food to the needy or offering insurance.

Many benevolent associations consisted of people who came from the same European town. These organizations were called *landsmanschaften*, a Yiddish word that means "group of fellow countrymen." These townsmen regrouped in the United States and attended gatherings to reminisce about the "old country," speak their native language, and provide mutual support. Almost every immigrant group in the late 19th century formed benevolent and social organizations whose purpose was to maintain cultural ties to their countries, cities, and/or towns of origin. For Jewish immigrants, the *landsmanschaft* created the mechanism necessary to assimilate into American society.

But by the end of the 19th century, the Jewish community found that these smaller agencies and associations were not strong enough to provide for the needs of a growing immigrant population. In fact, there were so many different groups that the people in the Jewish community began to tire of the many volunteers who came to their doors asking for donations. The various groups were competing with one another for charitable donations.

The solution to these problems was found in an organizational structure called a federation. The leaders of the Boston Jewish community decided to bring all the Jewish charitable organizations of their city under one single organizational umbrella. In that city, the result was an organization called the Federated Jewish Charities of Boston. In 1896, the Jewish community in Cincinnati, Ohio, also federated its charitable organizations under one umbrella. Today there are 189 Jewish federations across the United States.

Federations operate under the principle that all social service agencies within a city should maintain their independence, while at the same time use one another as resources for information and fundraising. The organized Jewish community found that wealthy community members preferred to be approached for charitable donations by a single person or through a single event each year. Therefore, all the agencies formed a federation through which they organized a yearly fundraiser. Once the funds were collected, the agencies met

THE INDUSTRIAL REMOVAL OFFICE

In the 1890s, at the height of the Massive Eastern European immigration, the United Hebrew Charities, the Baron de Hirsch Fund, B'nai B'rith, and other agencies sponsored a program called the Industrial Removal Office. The idea was to direct new Jewish immigrants to move into the American interior.

Jewish leaders feared the congestion in the cities created so many social problems that the American government might be forced to stop Eastern European immigration. Therefore, programs coming from the Industrial Removal Office were designed to convince new Jewish immigrants to move to states such as Ohio, and to help them make the move.

Some Jewish communities, such as the one in Cincinnati, can trace their history to the Industrial Removal Office. While the intention was good, the outcome of the program was not successful. Most new Jewish settlements in the west did not last very long, and the congestion in eastern cities was not eased very much.

together to decide how much money each independent agency would receive from the main pot. In addition to fund-raising, agencies shared experiences so that all agencies knew what kind of programs would work and what kind of programs would not.

The federated system seemed to work well for the growing American Jewish community by protecting different group interests within the community. The federated system reflected the American idea of individualism. Each social welfare agency had developed with its own character and sense of independence; they did not wish to be swallowed up by a larger organization.

Jewish federations were successful in the United States because of their commitment to religious pluralism and the unique individual nature of their member agencies. This meant that Jews who believed in different interpretations of Judaism could work together to achieve a common goal: caring for the welfare of the American Jewish people.

The federation idea emerged from European ideas of Jewish community. However, many characteristics of federations, such as independence and democracy, were distinctly American. In fact, the Jewish model of federation was to be copied by one of the largest charitable organizations in American history: the United Way. Catholic Charities, today the largest private social service organization in America, also borrowed the federation idea from the American Jewish community.

The American Labor Movement

The working conditions in New York City at the end of the 19th century and the beginning of the 20th were horrible. The Jewish immigrants were not farmers, because in most of Eastern Europe they had been forbidden to own land. Instead, they were usually tradesmen or tailors. Most of them found jobs working for merchants or in small factories, often in the garment industry. The shops they worked in were airless, dark, and unsafe. Often the toilets were outside the building, but the doors were locked so the workers could not take a break even to go to the bathroom.

Many Jewish immigrant workers labored over their tools and cloth for 65 to 75 hours a week, for little pay. They often had to provide their own tools, including sewing machines, and they also paid for their own chairs and lockers. When they damaged a garment in the process of making it, they paid for that, as well. Sometimes, the workers had to pay their supervisors for the right to work.

THE GALVESTON PLAN

In 1906, Congress established Galveston, Texas, as an entry port for immigrants. (Entry ports were places where immigrants could receive a required medical examination and be formally admitted into the United States.) Jacob Schiff, a successful banker, financier, philanthropist, and American Jew, sponsored a program that diverted ships loaded with Jewish immigrants from New York to Galveston, before they even stepped onto American soil.

The aim of the program, like the Industrial Removal Office, was to encourage immigrants to settle in less crowded areas.

However, many Jewish immigrants did not want to live in Texas. They had friends and family in New York, and they wanted to settle there. Only 10,000 Jewish immigrants settled in Galveston in the seven years of the plan.

There were few rules governing the treatment of laborers and there was no person or agency to protect them. The garment industry was able to get people to work for them under these appalling conditions because there were so many new immigrants who needed jobs.

Labor unions developed as the 19th century ended and the 20th century began. These organizations were committed to improving working conditions by uniting workers so that their demands would carry more weight with the employers. Individually, workers could not effect change because if they quit their job, someone else would quickly take their place. But when the workers decided as a group not to work, an action called a strike, they were able to force business owners to improve their working conditions.

A labor union called the Workmen's Circle, founded in 1892, was a long-lasting, effective organization. The Workmen's Circle provided insurance and mutual aid. For example, if a person was injured on the job, the Workmen's Circle would pay them money until they recovered. It also sponsored lectures and discussions that circulated ideas about fair labor practices, such as limiting a work day to eight hours.

Jewish Labor Groups

In the first decade of the 20th century, many Russian Jews were involved in a political movement called socialism. Feeling disconnected from mainstream Russian culture, many Jews found the communal nature of socialism attractive. Socialism also offered a plan to redress the terrible economic inequality among the rich and poor in Russia, and this appealed to the Jewish sense of *tzedakah*.

These Russian Jewish socialists called their political party the Bund. As the massive immigration of Jews from Eastern Europe, which included Russia, continued, many immigrants brought their socialist ideas with them to the United States. These ideas included fair labor practices and better wages for workers.

Morris Hillquit (1869–1933) was born in Latvia (then part of Russia) and came to America when he was 17 years old. He brought with him the socialist dream of a fair and equal society. In 1888, Hillquit was among the Jewish leaders who formed the United Hebrew Trades, a labor union. He was joined by a 19-year-old shirtmaker and a member of the Bund named Bernard Weinstein, and many others. Hillquit won the respect of those he represented, and became a spokesman for the workers.

PIECEWORK
Also called "by the piece," this meant workers were paid only for the work they completed. For example, if their job was to sew shirts, they got a small amount of money for each shirt they completed. This way of paying workers forces people to work long hours to earn enough to live on.

Better work rules
Jewish labor groups applied their political and social ideals to labor relations, fighting for better conditions for all workers. These women are on strike in the 1920s.

Hillquit noted in his autobiography, *Loose Leaves from a Busy Life* (1934), "There were hundreds of middlemen in the clothing industry, in fierce competition with one another. A number of hired sewing machines set up in a tenement-house room, often connected with their own living quarters, constituted their establishment. In these dark, ill-ventilated, and unsanitary shops, a welter of working and perspiring humanity, men and women, were crowded together. Their pay was nominal, their work hours unlimited. As a rule they were employed 'by the piece,' and, as their work was seasonal and irregular, they were spurred to inhuman exertions. They were weak from overwork and malnutrition, tired and listless, meek and submissive. Tuberculosis, the dread plague of the tenements, was rife among them."

In 1890, Joseph Barondess (1867–1928), a Jewish immigrant, organized a strike of cloak makers, who were the largest group of workers in the garment industry. Barondess made passionate speeches about the rights of workers, and he used references to Jewish literature to support his opinions. Three thousand cloak makers participated in the 1890 strike, despite police brutality, economic losses, and hunger. The strike resulted in a temporary reduction of hours and workload. A small battle had been won, but the war continued.

The United Hebrew Trades and the Workmen's Circle were given a platform to express their ideas and call the workers to action by the newspaper *The Jewish Daily Forward*. This popular paper reported on and discussed the lectures provided by organizations like the Workmen's Circle. It brought thousands of Jewish laborers together and provided a forum for ideas and goals. Together the Jewish labor unions and the *Forward* worked to alleviate the terrible plight of immigrant workers.

Jewish involvement in the trade union movements, and in the ownership of many garment businesses, helped advance the acceptance of labor unions in the United States. Between 1913 and 1916, many strikes were held that gained significant improvements for workers, and in 1916 there were more than 250,000 labor union members in the United States. By the time of the Great Depression (in the early 1930s), the idea of labor unions had become a part of American culture.

In 1932, the president of the International Ladies Garment Workers Union, a Russian Jewish immigrant named David Dubinsky, supported Franklin D. Roosevelt's bid for the presidency and his efforts to formulate the New Deal—a package of programs to help Americans pull out of the poverty the Depression had wrought. In 1935, the National Labor Relations Act was enacted by Congress. It guaranteed workers the right to join unions without fear of management reprisal. It also created the National Labor Relations Board to enforce this right, and prohibited employers from committing unfair labor practices that might discourage organizing or prevent workers from negotiating a union contract.

20th-Century Social Change

The two World Wars of the 20th century shaped the nature of American Jewish philanthropy and social welfare. After a wave of pogroms—violent attacks on whole communities of Jews in Russia—American Jews like Jacob Schiff began to raise money to save Jews from violence in Russia. In 1906 they formed the American Jewish Committee, an organization committed to defending Jews around the world. The American Jewish Committee was made up mostly of German Jews. It remains an effective voice for Jewish rights, even today.

In 1914, after the start of World War I, the American Jewish Committee organized a meeting of 39 American Jewish organizations to discuss the dangers Jews faced around the world. The result of this meeting was a union of all different types of Jews in America—German, Eastern European, socialist, Orthodox, and Reform.

SAMUEL GOMPERS

Another Jewish immigrant, Samuel Gompers (1850–1924), provided strong leadership to the union movement. Gompers was the first president of the American Federation of Labor (AFL) in 1886. He did not rely on visions of a worker's paradise, where management and labor would work hand in hand. He believed poor working conditions were a direct result of the conflict of interest between management and labor that is inherent in capitalism. He worked to change these conditions through unionization and collective bargaining—negotiations between an employer and union officials who represent all the workers.

The United Hebrew Trades supported the American Federation of Labor, thus securing the collective success of Jewish workers' demands for better work conditions. Gompers and his American Federation of Labor also organized the International Ladies Garment Workers Union (ILGWU), a collaboration of cloak makers, pressers, cutters, and shirtwaist makers.

A Terrible Fire

On March 25, 1911, a fire broke out at the Triangle Shirtwaist Company factory. Even though the company's owners had promised better working conditions and half days on Saturday, they had not fulfilled the agreement. Many scraps of oily cloth littered the floor, the steel doors leading to the bathrooms were locked, and the fire exits were either locked or blocked by machinery. When someone carelessly dropped a lit cigarette on the floor, a fire spread quickly throughout the building.

The owners raced out of the building without unlocking the doors, and the women working inside were unable to get out. Many of the women jumped from the windows, others suffocated or were burned. In all, 147 women and 21 men died, and another 200 people were injured.

Later called the Triangle Fire, the horrifying event catalyzed more than 100,000 workers to band together to demand better working conditions. The irony of the situation is that in many factories, Jewish owners were exploiting Jewish workers. The Triangle Fire forced many of these wealthy Jews to re-examine the way they were running their factories.

Joseph Schaffner, a Jewish philanthropist and business owner, was one factory owner who changed his life after the Triangle Fire. He forced his business partners to agree to improve working conditions in their factories.

The tragedy of the Triangle Fire motivated all labor unions, Jewish and non-Jewish alike, to pull together and create lasting change in American labor practices.

Together they established the American Jewish Joint Distribution Committee, often called simply the Joint. The Joint was responsible for distributing the funds raised by American Jews. Around the world, the Joint rescued Jews in danger and provided supplies to places where Jews were in need, such as Russia, Austria, Germany, and Palestine.

The needs of the Jewish community in the 1920s motivated the formation of the Jewish Welfare Funds. These funds, unlike the international funds of the Joint, were used to meet the needs of American Jews. The Jewish Welfare Funds were often associated with a local Jewish federation.

In 1932, Jewish federations across the United States formed the Council of Jewish Federations and Welfare Funds (CJFWF). The CJFWF provided an umbrella organization through which federations could share successes and failures, collect information about Jewish communities throughout the country, and otherwise focus the efforts of American Jewish communities. However, the CJFWF did not have the authority to control each local federation. Thus, the autonomy of each local federation was protected, and each federation now could learn from the experiences of Jewish communities across the United States.

The Great Depression

In the first three decades of the 20th century, Jewish social services, often connected to a federation, prided themselves on maintaining very high standards, such as individual attention and providing special services like kosher food baskets.

Before the Great Depression of the 1930s, the federal government did not pay for social welfare programs. Instead, religious groups and private charitable organizations ran many programs, along with some state and city relief. But the Depression was so severe that these private, state, and city programs could not take care of all of those in need, and the federal government became involved. President Roosevelt's New Deal included many programs to help the poor and unemployed.

It became clear to Jewish, Protestant, Catholic, and other private agencies that their efforts to provide relief to the poor, sick, and unemployed were not enough. Jewish federations supported the growth of federal aid in the United States, and many Jewish agencies saw it as their duty to be an example of high-quality service that the government could use as a model. In fact, the Jewish community felt that through their example, public welfare programs were forced to provide quality care.

Henry Monsky, the first vice president of the Jewish Community Center and Welfare Federation in Omaha, Nebraska, (who later became president of B'nai Brith) wrote in the March 1932 issue of *Jewish Social Service Quarterly* ("The Integration of the Jewish with the General Community"), "With pardonable pride, I think, we may claim that the social work standards of Jewish agencies have in a number of activities been of a higher order than those of non-Jewish agencies. A standardization of practice and procedure in all social work of a given community is much to be desired. This is said in the hope that our standards may be maintained and met by the other agencies, budgets permitting. The Jewish group, as a part of the community, must therefore give its fullest measure of cooperation. It is our task; it is our duty, to bring our people to the realization of how essential and indispensable social work is to the community."

The Federations Evolve

After World War II, the needs of Jewish communities changed. Many of the Jews who had needed relief aid in the 1900s and during the Great Depression in the 1930s had become middle-class Americans by the end of the war. They no longer needed an agency to provide for their basic needs. Many American Jews owned their own businesses or had found success in professions such as medicine and law.

There was certainly still a need for Jewish social welfare agencies, especially just after World War II when many refugees of the Holocaust immigrated to America. But the vast majority of American Jews had become financially secure, and they began to look elsewhere for their charitable work.

The Joint Distribution Committee and the United Palestine Appeal combined to form the United Jewish Appeal in 1938, after Kristallnacht (see page 53) signaled a heightened degree of anti-Semitism in Germany. The purpose of the United Jewish Appeal was to raise money to rescue the victims of World War II and victims of anti-Semitism around the world.

After Hitler was defeated in 1944, the magnitude of the Holocaust became clear. Many Jews no longer wished to remain in Europe, but they had nowhere else to go where they would be guaranteed the right to stay and build a new life. Many governments, as they had demonstrated during the war, did not want to allow millions of Jews to enter their countries. And so the world acknowledged the need for a Jewish homeland, and the state of Israel became a reality in 1948.

The philosophical and theological excitement surrounding the establishment of Israel inspired American Jews across the United States to donate money to support the new nation, in addition to the funds they were already donating to alleviate the suffering of what was left of European Jewry after the Holocaust.

In 1967, the 19-year-old state of Israel was attacked by its neighbors, in what came to be known as the Six Day War. Israel won the war quickly, but at a high cost. In the United States, the federations and the United Jewish Appeal received more donations from more people than they had in all the years before.

It became clear that the American Jewish community was committed to the federation idea. For many Jews in the United States, supporting the Jewish federations and the United Jewish Appeal became part of their identity as Jews. They were committed to the survival of the Jewish people, and they were committed to ensuring the safety and security of all Jews around the world.

Helping Out Today

In the last decades of the 20th century, Jewish federations found themselves dealing with new issues never imagined by the founders of the federations. Instead of assisting millions of poor, unemployed immigrants, the American Jewish community has turned to important family issues, such as divorce, disabled children, addiction, and old age.

Most local Jewish communities have some kind of Jewish family agency, supported, in part, by the federations. For example, in Greenwich, Connecticut, the agency that handles family issues is Jewish Family Services. In Boston, Massachusetts, the Jewish family agency is called Jewish Children and Family Services. These organizations often provide counseling for parents and children, care for the elderly, and organize after-school programs for children.

Sometimes these organizations are asked by local governments to serve a larger group of people. In Boston, Jewish Children and Family Service runs an after-school program for all inner city children, whether or not they are Jewish.

Many federation agencies serve groups of people other than Jews. They do this for several reasons. First, the Jewish concepts of *ohr l'goyim* (a light for nations) and *tikkun olam* (building a better world) encompass all people, not just Jews. Jews believe it is their responsibility to provide a strong, positive example of how people should treat one another. In addition, Jewish social welfare agencies often run programs very well—so well that federal and local agencies sometimes find it more efficient to simply ask these agencies to increase the scope of their programs.

In 1989, the Association of Jewish Family and Children's Agencies found that 72 of 75 agencies across the United States were serving non-Jewish clients in some fashion. This expansion of services enables Jewish family agencies to reach out to the surrounding community—an activity that encourages good relations between Jews and non-Jews and provides opportunities for the Jewish community to live the ideal of *ohr l'goyim*.

EVERY EFFORT MATTERS
These children in Chicago are selling *challah*, a special Sabbath bread, to raise money for their local Jewish Community Center programs.

National and Political Impact of Jews and Judaism

5

EARLY JEWISH POLITICAL POWER IN AMERICA CAME BY WAY OF business. As America became increasingly industrialized, the political clout once enjoyed by farmers was transferred to railroad owners and manufacturers. A large number of Jewish Americans were prominent in various industries, and they used this wealth and power to try to influence the national scene.

Railroads were among the most important industries in which Jewish men had a hand—mainly in financing their construction. By the 19th century, a network of railroads connected the East Coast of the United States with the West Coast. Because of the railroads, cities such as Chicago, Omaha, and Kansas City grew and fortunes were made. The new millionaires became charter members of what was referred to as The Gilded Age. Members of The Gilded Age enjoyed lavish lifestyles.

This exclusive group included Jay Gould, Edward Harriman, and J.P. Morgan. Jewish industrialists joined the group as well, including Joseph Seligman, who started out as a peddler and became one of the most important bankers in America, and Abraham Kuhn and Solomon Loeb, founders of the banking firm Kuhn, Loeb, and Co.

Powerful Men and Families

Shortly after arriving in the United States in early 1837, Joseph Seligman (1819–1880) began walking from New York to Mauch Chunk, Pennsylvania, where his mother had a relative. There he got a job with Asa Packer, a canal boat builder. During the Civil War, Seligman's brother William bought a clothing factory, and after winning a Union contract, the two brothers manufactured uniforms for Union soldiers. However, the Union government did not have cash to pay them for the uniforms, preferring instead to pay with bonds. Joseph Seligman accepted the bonds and began selling them in Europe. Some historians have suggested that Seligman's bond-selling efforts were crucial to the Union victory.

By the end of the Civil War, Seligman had established a banking house in New York with offices in Paris, London, San Francisco, and New Orleans, modeled after the Rothschild House of Banking in Europe. Using his powerful connections in the financial world, he became involved with the growth of the railroad industry.

Jacob Schiff (1847–1920), the son-in-law of Solomon Loeb, was another German-Jewish immigrant with ties to commercial banking and railroad expansion. Born in Frankfurt, Schiff's father was a stockbroker. Through family friends, Schiff met Kuhn, who introduced him to Loeb, who hired him at their banking firm.

Soon Schiff became a railroad specialist. He rode the various lines and spoke with engineers, porters, and anyone else who would help him to become more than just an investment advisor. Schiff's goal was to become a manager. Working with and competing against other leaders in the industry led Schiff's firm to become the largest Jewish-owned investment banking firm. The firm was also involved in the mining industry and worked for the Guggenheim family to acquire the American Smelting and Refining Company.

Originally from Switzerland, the Guggenheim family settled in Pennsylvania, where they were in the business of importing and distributing a variety of household items. They also owned a factory in Switzerland where lace was manufactured.

As the family business grew, Meyer Guggenheim (1828-1905), together with fellow businessman Charles Graham, acquired a one-third share of two lead and silver mines near Leadville, Colorado. Knowing nothing about mining, Guggenheim went to Colorado to inspect his investment. Unexpectedly, silver and copper were found, leading Guggenheim to bring two of his sons to Leadville to study metallurgy.

Bernard Baruch (1870–1965), a mining investor who would later become a presidential advisor, led the Guggenheims to Richard Gatling, the inventor of a smelting process. Using Gatling's process, the family invested in additional smelters in Colorado and Mexico. Forming a family trust fund, they bought mines in Bolivia, Alaska, Africa, and Chile, becoming an international mining giant and making the family both powerful and wealthy. Historians have credited Meyer Guggenheim with laying the foundation for the United States copper industry.

From Germany to Washington

German Jews demonstrated their loyalty to the United States by becoming active in politics. Prominent German-Jewish leaders participated in Republican Party politics in Chicago, Cincinnati, San Francisco, and Philadelphia. Lucius Littauer (1859–1944), for example, was a millionaire glove maker from New York. A graduate of Harvard University, he had no difficulty asking his fellow Harvard graduate and friend, President Theodore Roosevelt, to intercede on behalf of Jewish communities in Europe. Littauer contributed generously to Harvard, establishing the Littauer School of Public Administration and the Littauer Chair of Jewish Studies. Loyalties in the German-Jewish community switched to the Democratic Party with the election of Woodrow Wilson.

Throughout American history, a significant number of Jewish professionals have entered government service, serving as advisors to the president. Outstanding among this group of distinguished men are Louis Marshall, Bernard Baruch, and Herbert Lehman.

A millionaire at age 30, Bernard Baruch served several American presidents with distinction. Fascinated with the political process and governmental affairs, Baruch was a generous member of the Democratic Party. When Wilson was elected president, he invited Baruch to join the White House staff. During World War I, Wilson appointed him to the Advisory Commission to the Council of National Defense. Accepting this appointment, Baruch resigned his previously held positions and sold his seat on the Stock Exchange.

After the war, he accompanied Wilson to the Versailles peace conference. Baruch continued his role as advisor to Presidents Warren Harding, Herbert Hoover, and Franklin Roosevelt. During World War II, he was involved in a variety of projects on behalf of the American

BOND
A certificate issued by a government or a public company, promising to repay borrowed money within a specific time at a fixed rate of interest.

Elder statesman
Bernard Baruch served as
an advisor and confidant to
five American presidents.

government, and after the war, President Harry Truman appointed him
to the United Nations Atomic Energy Commission. His later years were
spent as a highly respected elder statesman.

Born in Syracuse, New York, Louis Marshall (1856–1929) became
the chief spokesman for matters concerning Jewish Americans. Trained
as an attorney, Marshall specialized in Constitutional and corporate
law, arguing many cases before the U.S. Supreme Court. When Leo
Frank was charged with the murder of a Georgia factory girl (see the
box on page 93), the defending attorney was Marshall.

After World War I he played a key role as mediator as part of the
Jewish delegation to the Paris Peace Conference, where he supported
granting national minority rights to the Jews of Eastern European
states. His intervention at Harvard University helped overturn a decision to limit the number of qualified Jewish students.

Herbert Lehman (1878–1963) was born in New York City, the son of German-Jewish immigrants, and entered the family investment banking business after graduating from college. While serving as a textile procurement specialist with the navy during World War I, Lehman befriended future president Franklin D. Roosevelt.

After the war, Lehman became active in politics, supporting Democratic presidential candidate Alfred E. Smith. He eventually became chairman of the finance committee of the Democratic National Committee. His friendship with Roosevelt led him to run as lieutenant governor when Roosevelt successfully ran for governor of New York in 1928. Lehman was elected governor of New York in 1932—the same year Roosevelt was elected president.

American Jews and Israel

In the late 1880s, as life grew worse for Eastern European Jews, the situation for Jews living in Western Europe also deteriorated. The date was January 5, 1895, and the place was Paris, France. Alfred Dreyfus, a Jewish captain in the French army, was falsely accused of revealing military secrets. Despite his innocence, he was publicly denounced, and sentenced to solitary confinement on Devil's Island. As Dreyfus was being led away, the crowd chanted, "Death to the traitor! Death to the Jews!" This experience proved to be life-altering for one member of the press corps covering the trial—Theodor Herzl (1860–1904).

Herzl, a university graduate with a degree in law, was a secular Jew; that is, he did not consider himself to be a religious man. But living in Vienna, he became sensitive to the hardships and limitations placed on Jews. The Dreyfus trial motivated him to take action.

Herzl understood that Jews could never live completely as Jews, secular or religious, unless they had their own state. In his book, *The Jewish State*, he wrote, "We are a people, a people. Everywhere we have tried honestly to disappear in the surrounding community, and to retain only the faith of our fathers. We are not permitted to do it. In vain do we show our loyalty, and in some places an exaggerated patriotism; in vain do we bring the same sacrifices of blood and gold as our fellow-citizens; in vain do we exert ourselves to increase the glory of our fatherlands by achievements in art and science." In this book, Herzl outlined a plan that created a movement called Zionism.

At the First World Zionist Congress, held in Basel, Switzerland,

A LYNCHING IN ATLANTA

In 1913, Leo Frank was convicted of murdering Mary Phagan, a 13-year-old employee of the Atlanta pencil factory that Frank managed. Even after Frank's housekeeper said he was at home at the time of the murder, and, despite the fact that the janitor at the factory had been seen washing blood off his shirt, Frank was convicted. Facing incredible pressure from the people of Atlanta, the judge sentenced Frank to death.

After a review of the evidence, and even a recommendation from the original trial judge, Georgia Governor Frank Slaton changed the sentence to life in prison. Soon after, on August 17, 1915, a group of 25 men stormed the prison hospital where Frank was recovering from having his throat slashed by another inmate. They kidnapped Frank, drove him more than 100 miles to Mary Phagan's hometown of Marietta, Georgia, and hanged him from a tree. Townsfolk were proudly photographed beneath Frank's swinging corpse.

Prominent Jewish Politicians

The Jewish tradition of public service through political activism led many Jews to a life in government. David Yulee of Florida was the first Jew to serve in the United States Senate, in 1845; Judah Benjamin represented Louisiana from 1853 to 1861. Others who rose to Cabinet-level positions included Secretary of Commerce and Labor Oscar Straus (who served from 1906 to 1909), Secretary of the Treasury Henry Morgenthau (who served from 1934 to 1945), Secretary of Labor Arthur Goldberg (who served from 1961 to 1962), and Secretary of State Henry Kissinger (who served from 1973 to 1977).

Supreme Court Justices include Louis D. Brandeis, Benjamin Cardozo, Felix Frankfurter, Arthur Goldberg, Abraham Fortas, and, on the current Court, Ruth Bader Ginzburg, and Steven Breyer.

Senators Jacob Javits of New York and Abraham Ribicoff of Connecticut were, for a time, among the most powerful politicians in the nation. Other Jewish senators include Barbara Boxer, Dianne Feinstein, Joseph Lieberman, Carl Levin, Arlen Specter, Paul Wellstone, Russ Feingold, Herbert Kohl, Ron Wyden, Frank Lautenberg, .and Charles Schumer. A large number of Jews serve in the House of Representatives, including Nita Lowey, Eric Cantor, Jane Haman, Steve Israel, Adam Schiff, and many others.

ZIONISM

An international movement calling for the establishment of a Jewish state in Palestine. It comes from the word Zion, which was the hill in Jerusalem where King David (see page 10) built his city.

---

in August 1897, Herzl called on Jews to work toward the establishment of a Jewish state. The goal of the meeting was to lay the framework for the Zionist movement. Among the Americans attending the Congress were Rosa Sonnenschein and Adam Rosenberg. Rosenberg addressed the delegates on the state of American Jewry; Sonnenschein attended as a journalist representing *The American Jewess*, a magazine for Jewish-American women that she founded and edited.

Louis D. Brandeis, the Supreme Court justice, was also convinced that Jews would disappear unless there was a Jewish homeland. At an address delivered at the conference of the Eastern Council of Reform Rabbis in June 1915, he said, "Let no American imagine that Zionism is inconsistent with patriotism. To be good Americans, we must be better Jews, and to be better Jews, we must become Zionists."

The Zionist movement gained strength and support as the persecution of Jews in Europe accelerated. Supporters believed that if there had been a Jewish state, millions would not have been killed by Hitler and his Nazi machine. When efforts urging politicians to take action on behalf of Holocaust victims were unsuccessful, Zionists turned their efforts instead toward American Jews.

During World War II, membership in American Zionist organizations grew from 49,000 to more than 250,000, with Hadassah as the largest constituency. American Zionists were also active selling American war bonds; more than $68 million was raised during the war.

In 1947, as thousands of Jewish Holocaust survivors languished in displaced persons camps in Europe, a plan was presented to the United Nations. Called the Partition Plan, it called for the division of Palestine into two states: one for Jews and the other for Arabs. Zionists supported this plan, hoping that the world would agree. President Truman ordered the American delegation to the United Nations to vote in favor of the plan. And on May 14, 1948, when the state of Israel was officially proclaimed, Truman was the first to recognize the new state. To thank the president for this bold step, Israel's first president, Chaim Weizmann, later presented Truman with a Torah scroll.

Within hours of announcing the establishment of the state, Is-

Hadassah

Henrietta Szold (1860–1945) founded Hadassah, the largest Jewish women's organization in the world. The name is taken from the Hebrew name of Queen Esther, the heroine of Purim (see page 17).

Born in Baltimore, Szold first visited Palestine in 1909. She was appalled at the widespread illness and poverty. Jews and Arabs suffered from trachoma and malaria. Their surroundings were unsanitary and unsafe. There were no doctors or nurses to care for the sick. Szold returned home with the goal of organizing an agency to provide health aid in Palestine.

Lotta Levensohn, who served as secretary to Dr. Judah Magnus at the Federation of American Zionists, wrote in her memoirs, *Vision and Fulfillment* (1950), "After her trip to Palestine in 1909, Miss Szold presented to us a plan for district visiting nursing patterned after Lillian Wald's project on the East Side of New York. It was only after two years of planning and preparation that a meeting was called on February 24, 1912, in the vestry rooms of Temple Emanu-El in New York for the formation of a country-wide women's Zionist organization with the twin purposes of Zionist education in America and a specific health project in Palestine."

Hadassah's doctors and nurses, wearing red stars of David, went to Palestine to help in 1918. From this modest beginning, Hadassah grew into the largest women's Zionist organization in the world. Its partnership with the Hebrew University has created a medical center in Jerusalem that is one of the top hospitals and medical and dental schools in the Middle East.

In 1933, Szold turned her attention to the children who survived the Holocaust, rallying Hadassah members to contribute generously to Youth Aliyah—an organization that provided housing, education, and vocational training to thousands of children.

Today, Hadassah supports medical research and provides educational programs throughout the world. Hadassah's medical facilities never turn away anyone in need of assistance.

Birth of a nation
American Jews gathered outside the Israeli embassy in Washington, D.C., on May 14, 1948, to celebrate as the flag of Israel was raised for the first time.

rael's neighbors on every border attacked. Jewish Americans, through the Joint Distribution Committee, immediately began sending money, food, clothing, and medical supplies. At the same time, they called on the U.S. government to support Israel with loans and foreign aid.

During Israel's early years, Jewish Americans were called on many times. Jewish American pilots risked their lives to bring arms and supplies to Israel. Others fought bravely in the 1948 War of Independence alongside Israeli soldiers. And some Jewish Americans assisted by raising money for ships that brought immigrants to Israel. One of the most famous of these ships was the *Exodus*, the subject of a novel of the same name by Leon Uris. The *Exodus*, holding thousands of refugees, was captured by British soldiers, who sent them back to displaced persons camps. A movie was made of the book, starring Paul Newman.

Since 1948, the state of Israel has welcomed millions of Jews, as tourists and as citizens. Each year, thousands of American teens travel to Israel to learn about their history and culture. Many Americans have spent time working on collective settlements called *kibbutzim*, while others study in world-class institutions, including the Hebrew University of Jerusalem and the Technion in Haifa. In return, many Israeli teens travel to the United States and other countries. Bringing Americans and Israelis together has promoted greater understanding and friendship.

American Zionists continue to defend Israel and support the state in its quest for peaceful relations with its Arab neighbors. They value and celebrate Israeli achievements in medical research and technology. And they raise loud voices to protest unfair representation of current events in the printed media and on television. Many Jewish Americans believe that while life in the United States is wonderful, Israel is the only place where, as Jews, they can live most meaningfully.

The Civil Rights Movement

Civil rights is one issue of national importance in which Jewish participation has been crucial. Acting on the core principal of Jewish ethics that demands justice and compassion for all people, Jewish leaders have stood in the forefront to ensure civil rights for all Americans.

Rabbi Stephen Wise of New York and Rabbi Emil Hirsch of Chicago, together with Lillian Wald, Henry Moskowitz, Joel and Arthur Spingarn, Martha Gruening, and Herbert Seligman, were among those who helped organize the National Association for the Advancement of Colored People (NAACP) in 1909. Arthur Spingarn served in the association's legal department beginning in 1913, and remained its unpaid director for 25 years. From 1940 to 1966, he served as president of the NAACP. Jacob Schiff, Felix Warburg, and the Rosenwald family were major contributors to the NAACP. According to NAACP leader Roy Wilkens, "Jewish people understand this business of discrimination; they have great sympathy for those who are fighting it."

In the summers of 1965 and 1966, Peter Geffen traveled to South Carolina to work for the Southern Community Organization and Political Education Project. Geffen's goal was to assist poor black farmers so that they would be able to pass the reading test then required to become registered voters.

Rabbi Charles Mantinband served as rabbi in congregations in Alabama, Mississippi, and Texas, where he became well-known for his support of equal rights for all people. As a member of the Southern

GOLDA MEIR

One of the most important people in the history of Israel had strong American roots. Golda Meir (1898–1978) was born in Russia, and came to America with her family in 1906. They settled in Milwaukee, Wisconsin. She completed her education, married Morris Myerson, and then decided to move to Palestine. Several years later, she began a political career. In 1946, she became the head of the political department of the Jewish Agency and was sent back to the United States to raise money for Israel. In 1969, Golda Meir, a former American schoolteacher, became Israel's prime minister.

Regional Council, Mantinband worked to improve white and black community relations in the South through action-based programs.

Another prominent rabbi, Abraham Joshua Heschel, was often seen marching arm-in-arm with Rev. Martin Luther King, Jr. "For many of us, the march from Selma to Montgomery [in 1965] was both protest and prayer," he wrote in *Insecurity and Freedom* (1996). "Even without words, our march was worship. I felt my legs were praying."

In the 1960s, hundreds of Jewish college students heard King's call and went to the south to register black voters. In the summer of 1964, two of these activists, Andrew Goodman and Michael Schwerner, disappeared, along with African-American civil rights worker James Chaney, in Meridian, Mississippi. They were later found murdered.

Other Jews also paid dearly, not only because of their participation in the civil rights movement, but also because of their Judaism. The Ku Klux Klan regularly attacked rabbis and Jewish lay leaders in their homes and synagogues. Several synagogues in the South were bombed after groups of rabbis joined marches for civil rights in Birmingham and Selma, Alabama.

David Dubinsky, president of the International Ladies' Garment Workers Union, led his union to taking a strong position in supporting

Comrades in arms
Rev. Martin Luther King, Jr., (center) and Rabbi Abraham Heschel (with the beard, on the far right of King) marched together many times in the fight for civil rights. Heschel said caring for others is a form of prayer.

Tense Times

Many books have been written about the relationship between Jews and African Americans. Some authors stress the strong ties between the two communities, based on their mutual quest for social justice, particularly during the civil rights movement, when prominent Jews marched with Rev. Martin Luther King, Jr. Other writers have described the less favorable relations between the two groups, including accusations of Jewish racism and Black anti-Semitism. Both these views are only part of the picture.

The complex relationship between the two communities came to a violent explosion in 1991 when Blacks and Hasidim rioted in the Crown Heights section of Brooklyn, New York, for four days. The incident that touched off the riots was an automobile accident in which a Black child, Gavin Cato, was hit and killed. Yankel Rosenbaum, a Hasidic rabbinical student from Australia, happened to be walking down the street when a gang of Black youths decided to retaliate and beat Rosenbaum to death.

Although much has been done during the past 10 years to build mutual respect between African American and Jewish community leaders, the relationship is still, at times, uneasy.

King and the civil rights movement. Jewish Americans marched in cities across the country to protest segregation and to demand equal rights. A 1966 study asked African Americans what group outside the Black community had done the most to help the civil rights movement, and Jews were on the top of the list.

Helping Other Jews

The tradition of helping one another has remained essential for Jewish Americans. Having achieved great success in America, many Jews have focused their attention on the needs of the worldwide Jewish community. In the 1970s and 1980s, the National Council for Soviet Jewry held rallies and demonstrations on behalf of Jews who were trapped in the Soviet Union. These Jews were forbidden to live as Jews, yet the Soviet government also refused to allow them to leave the country. Called *refusniks* when they applied for exit visas, many Jews openly challenged the Communist government and, as a result, were sent to prison.

Jewish Americans marched in Washington, D.C., New York, and other large cities to demand freedom for Anatoly Sheransky, Ida Nudel, and thousands of other *refusniks*. Finally, beginning in 1989, the floodgates opened and thousands of Soviet Jews were permitted to leave. The American Jewish community continued its fund-raising projects to ensure that once the refugees arrived in either the United States or Israel, they would find assistance to begin their lives again.

6

Important People in American Jewish History

Rabbi Sabato Morais (1823–1897)

Rabbi Sabato Morais was born in Livorno, Italy, into a "mixed" family representing both *ashkenazic* and *sephardic* traditions. Livorno (or Leghorn, as English sailors called it) was one of Europe's most important and vibrant Jewish communities. Since the late 16th century, Livorno offered a safe haven for Jews fleeing persecution.

Morais attended a new Jewish educational institution in Livorno that provided students with practical and religious instruction, secular and Jewish education. He was tutored in general studies at the University of Pisa and received rabbinical training in Livorno. This combination served him well when he immigrated to America in 1851. Living in many worlds, he was an observant Jew and a proud American citizen.

Morais represented a new style of Jewish leader: He dressed in modern clothes, yet he observed Jewish laws and traditions. A rabbi who loved music and poetry, he courageously spoke out on the issues confronting his own congregants at Philadelphia's Spanish and Portuguese synagogue, as well as on the problems of non-Jews in his community.

Morais emerged as a strong community leader. In articles that were published in the Jewish and general press, he opposed social and economic injustice, religious intolerance, and racial oppression. He was outspoken against slavery and restrictive immigration laws. During the Civil War, he was forced to remain quiet after receiving a gag order from his congregation because he was so outspoken in support of President Abraham Lincoln and the Union cause.

Recognizing that American Jews needed leadership to keep them connected to traditional Jewish values and customs, he supported early reformers. In addition to his rabbinical duties, he served as a professor of Bible studies at Maimonides College, the first American rabbinical seminary, which lasted only a short time in Philadelphia. After breaking with the Reform movement after a non-kosher meal was served at graduation ceremonies at Hebrew Union College, Morais turned his attention to the newly formed Conservative movement. He helped establish the Jewish Theological Seminary in 1887 in New York to train a new generation of traditional rabbis, and served as its first president until 1897.

Jacob Schiff (1847–1920)

Born in Frankfurt, Germany, Jacob Schiff was the son of a prominent German-Jewish family and a descendant of distinguished rabbis. After receiving both a secular and a religious education, he immigrated to America and quickly became a citizen. A successful businessman, Schiff played a leading role in accelerating American industrialization and was a prime mover in expanding the railroads.

Schiff was an investment banker and community leader who guided the American Jewish community from 1890 to 1920—the crucial years when more than 2 million Eastern European Jews arrived. He was a leading advocate for the Americanization of these immigrants, and worked hard to make sure they received the educational services they needed to learn English, as well as the skills necessary to integrate into American society.

Responding to the overwhelming number of immigrants arriving in New York, Schiff also pioneered the development of the Galveston Plan (see page 80).

Schiff also became a leader of the Reform movement in Judaism. However, relying on his more Orthodox upbringing, his love of the Jewish community led him to be a generous contributor to both the Conservative and Reform movements. In addition, he supported the Jewish Publication Society and helped establish the Jewish Division of the New York Public Library. After retiring from the brokerage firm bearing his name, he devoted his time and talents to Montefiore Hospital, where he served as president for 35 years.

It is interesting to note that while Schiff worked actively and tirelessly for the Jewish community, he was also involved in projects that benefited a broad range of people. He contributed funds to Harvard University, Barnard College, the American Red Cross, Tuskegee Institute, the Henry Street Settlement, and many other organizations.

Louis D. Brandeis (1856–1941)

Born in Louisville, Kentucky, into a family that celebrated both Jewish and Christian holidays and rituals, the young Brandeis was educated in Germany. He returned to the United States to attend Harvard Law School. After graduation, he became a successful lawyer and took an interest in politics. His was especially interested in public utilities and the trend of businesses to monopolize some of New England's most powerful companies. He was an outspoken opponent of the proposed merger of the Boston & Maine Railroad with the New York, New Haven, and Hartford Railroads. Recognized as a leader in the Democratic Party, he was a strong supporter of Woodrow Wilson, who was elected president in 1913. In 1916, Wilson appointed Brandeis a justice of the Supreme Court, the first Jew to hold the position.

Brandeis showed little interest in Jewish life or his own Jewish identity. However, this changed after he met Jacob de Hass, a British Jew from a Dutch sephardic family. De Hass had attended the first Zionist Congress in Basel, Switzerland, and had heard Theodor Herzl lay out his plan for a Jewish homeland in Palestine. At Herzl's suggestion, de Hass came to the United States as a representative of a Zionist organization. De Hass remained in the United States and became owner and editor of a local Jewish newspaper, the *Jewish Advocate*. It was in this position that de Hass met Brandeis and introduced him to Zionism.

As Brandeis learned more about the Zionist movement, he took on responsible positions in its leadership. His work for the movement had a profound affect on its organization and finances, because he was able to use his influence with the president and other important government officials to convince them that the only way Jews would survive was if a Jewish homeland was established in Palestine.

A FIDDLER IN AMERICA

Sholom Aleichem (1859–1916), the important Yiddish writer of short stories and plays, was born Solomon Rabinowitz in Russia. He adopted his pen name shortly after arriving in America. He is recognized all over the world as the author of *Fiddler on the Roof*.

Sholom Aleichem immigrated to the United States just before World War I. He became a frequent contributor to *The Jewish Daily Forward*, where his stories and satires were serialized. Sholom Aleichem is best known for his humor and for the way he was able to touch his readers' lives with his wonderful stories.

After becoming a Supreme Court justice, Brandeis switched to a behind-the-scenes role in the Zionist movement. In 1937, he convinced President Franklin Roosevelt to oppose a British plan to partition Palestine into several tiny states, and instead to support the idea of a Jewish national homeland. Brandeis wrote in "The Jewish Problem: How to Solve It" (quoted in *Brandeis on Zionism*, 1942), "To be a good American meant that local Jews should be Zionists."

Abraham Cahan (1860–1951)

Born in Vilna, Lithuania (then part of Russia), Abraham Cahan fled during the roundup of socialist revolutionaries that followed the assassination of Czar Alexander II. He eventually immigrated to the United States in 1892. Cahan settled on the Lower East Side of New York City, where he soon became a writer, lecturer, and editor for the socialist and labor movements. In 1897 when *The Jewish Daily Forward*, a

A vital link
Abraham Cahan's newspaper, The Jewish Daily Forward, *helped new immigrants keep in touch with one another and with the world around them.*

newspaper written entirely in Yiddish, first made its appearance on the streets of New York, Cahan was the editor-in-chief.

Funding to run the newspaper was raised through appeals to working people. In his memoirs, *The Education of Abraham Cahan* (published in English in 1969), Cahan describes one fund-raising session: "I shall never forget a mass meeting which we called in order to collect money for the proposed new paper. It was held in the large basement of the Valhallah Hall on Orchard Street. After the appeal we started the collections. I and another went around, our hats in hand, to collect the contributions. The audience responded generously, some donating ten-dollar, five-dollar, two-dollar bills and silver coins. People removed rings and wristwatches and threw them into the pile. I recall how heavy my hat became that I had to hold it with both hands so it should not rip open."

As editor, Cahan believed *The Forward* must "interest itself in the things that the masses are interested in when they aren't preoccupied with the daily struggle for bread." He made *The Forward* into a family newspaper, appealing to mothers and fathers, sisters and brothers, and any other relative who shared a room in the narrow tenement apartments where most immigrants lived. Written in simple Yiddish, *The Forward* addressed the problems faced by all immigrants. One of the most beloved columns was The Bintel Brief, one of America's first advice columns, to which thousands of readers would send in questions. (See page 42 for more about The Bintel Brief.)

Cahan is credited with providing a vehicle that offered Eastern European immigrants an opportunity to learn about American customs and culture. And while the paper never lost sight of its mission to provide services to the working class, it actually produced much more.

The Forward is still published, but in English now, and many of its readers, who are successful American leaders, are the descendants of the original readers.

Samuel Goldwyn (1882–1974)

Born in Poland, Samuel Gelbfisz came to the United States as a young teenager. His first job was sweeping floors in a glove manufacturing company, but he soon became a successful salesman. He entered the brand-new motion picture business with his brother-in-law, a well-

Movie mogul
Samuel Goldwyn became one of the most powerful movie producers in America, founding both MGM Studios and United Artists. Sir Laurence Olivier got his big break from Goldwyn.

known vaudevillian named Jesse Lasky, and a then-unknown director, Cecil B. DeMille. The three men collaborated to produce *The Squaw Man*, the first feature-length film made in Hollywood, It was a huge success.

Within two years, using his Americanized name, Goldfish, and the last syllable of his partners' (Edgar and Archibald Selwyn) last name, he formed Goldwyn Pictures Corporation. Soon after the formation of the company, Goldfish changed his last name to Goldwyn.

In 1923, Sam Goldwyn began to produce movies independently and started the MGM (Metro Goldwyn Mayer) movie studio. Later in his career he formed United Artists. Among the famous actors and actresses who worked for Goldwyn were Charlie Chaplin, Mary Pickford, and Douglas Fairbanks. He is credited with launching the careers of Ronald Coleman, Danny Kaye, Laurence Olivier, and many others. Among the movies he produced are *Wuthering Heights, The Secret Life of Walter Mitty*, and *Guys and Dolls*. In 1947, Goldwyn won an Academy Award for producing *The Best Years of Our Lives*, a film about the difficulties veterans of World War II faced when they returned home.

Rabbi Ahron Soloveichik (1918–2001)

A descendant of one of Europe's leading rabbinical dynasties, Rabbi Ahron Soloveichik was the founder and head of Yeshivas Brisk in Chicago, Illinois, and one of the world's most respected Talmudic scholars and authorities on Jewish law. Soloveichik was born in western Russia into a rabbinical dynasty going back nine generations. His equally famous brother, Rabbi Joseph Soloveichik, known as Rav and considered the 20th century's leading rabbinical scholar, was the head of Yeshiva University in New York.

The Soloveichik family came to the United States in 1930. Ahron Soloveichik graduated from Yeshiva College, where he received his rabbinical ordination. Finding it difficult to get a job in New York, he enrolled in New York University Law School. In 1966 he moved to Illinois, where he became head of the Hebrew Theological College in Skokie. And in 1974, he established the Yeshivas Brisk. While serving as head of that yeshiva, and despite partial paralysis caused by a stroke, Soloveichik flew to New York City every week to teach a Talmud class at Yeshiva University.

Throughout his career, Soloveichik was able to use his extensive knowledge of Jewish law and apply it to modern-day questions. In his obituary notice, his skill was called visionary; he was ruling on mat-

Superman's Creators

Symbolizing truth, justice, and the American way, Superman is, indeed, an American hero. But did you know he was created by Jerry Siegel and Joe Shuster, two Jewish Americans from Cleveland, Ohio?

Before the outbreak of World War II, Siegel and Shuster were working for DC Comics in New York. Together they dreamed up the idea of a superhero who came from another planet but grew up on Earth. Their editor liked the idea, and in June of 1938, volume 1 of *Action Comics* introduced Superman.

Superman could leap tall buildings in a single bound, deflect bullets, lift cars, rip metal doors from their hinges, and rescue women in distress. When the United States entered World War II, Superman became a combat hero. He destroyed Japanese submarines, Nazi armor, and any other wartime enemy advances.

Siegel and Shuster created Superman to reflect a core Jewish principal: To do good for its own sake and heal the world when one can. The fantasy of Superman has captivated Americans from the very first issue, and the authors' contribution to America's collective imagination has left an indelible mark.

ters concerning the use of stem cells more than 10 years ago. He was the only Orthodox rabbi in the United States to oppose the Vietnam War. He said sending young Americans to fight against Communism was an unrealistic goal.

Alan Greenspan (b.1926)

Born and raised in New York City, Alan Greenspan's first love was music. He studied at the Juilliard School of Music and took his first job as a clarinet and saxophone player in a swing band. Greenspan began his career in the world of finance as a stockbroker and retail worker, later becoming an economist. Together with William Townsend, he established the Townsend-Greenspan economic consulting firm

In 1967, Greenspan continued his career at the Federal Reserve Board. Greenspan's political career began in 1968 with an appointment by President Richard Nixon as director of policy research. President Gerald Ford named Greenspan his Chairman of Economic Advisers.

In 1987, President Ronald Reagan nominated Greenspan to the position of Chairman of the Federal Reserve Board, a position he has held since that time. As chairman of the Federal Reserve Board, Greenspan's job is to control monetary policies by determining short-term interest rates for American companies and consumers.

Joseph Lieberman (b.1942)

History was made on August 8, 2000, when Senator Joseph Lieberman was nominated as the Democratic Party's vice presidential candidate, running with Al Gore. Lieberman became the first Jewish American to be nominated for the White House. Born in Stamford, Connecticut, to a working-class Orthodox family, Lieberman has a reputation for being a politician who is not afraid to speak out on issues.

Lieberman entered state politics shortly after graduating Yale University. He served in the Connecticut State Senate, and in 1982 he was elected Connecticut's attorney general. In 1988 he was elected to the United States Senate. After losing the presidential election in 2000, Lieberman won back his Senate seat in a landslide victory.

Lieberman is a well-regarded man of principle and integrity. He has spoken out forcefully for human rights and encouraged more ethical behavior in government and among elected representatives. His criticism of President Bill Clinton's affair with Monica Lewinsky was

The King of Disney

Michael Eisner (b.1942) is Mickey Mouse's boss. Eisner is the chief executive officer of the Walt Disney Company, the enormous entertainment group. Eisner grew up in a family of successful businessmen and women. His great-grandfather, Sigmund Eisner, immigrated to the United States from Bohemia, Germany, and built a manufacturing company that made Boy Scout uniforms and military uniforms during World Wars I and II. Eisner's father, Lester, was a lawyer and entrepreneur who also administered the Department of Housing and Urban Development. His mother was an executive and co-founder of the American Safety Razor Company. Before becoming CEO of Disney, Michael Eisner worked for ABC and Paramount Pictures. He is one of the most important and influential figures in the entertainment industry.

widely admired as being forceful, eloquent, and to the point.

As an Orthodox Jew, Lieberman does not do business on the Sabbath. He will, however, attend key meetings and votes in the Congress on Saturday if his presence is required. Because Orthodox Jews are not allowed to drive on the Sabbath, he has often walked several miles to attend important meetings.

American Jews took great pride in the Democratic Party's nomination of Lieberman as Gore's running mate. It was as if a glass ceiling had been broken. After the announcement was made, Lieberman and Gore went to Lieberman's hometown of Stamford, Connecticut, to a throng of joyous supporters that included many people from the Jewish community. Later that evening, Lieberman attended services marking Tishah B'Av (a fast day commemorating the destruction of the temples that once stood in ancient Jerusalem) at Congregation Agudath Sholom in Stamford, which he had attended as a young man.

The Associated Press reported on August 7, 2000, that Jack Rosen, president of the American Jewish Congress, said, "Clearly the fact that a Jew is no longer an impediment to the highest office marks a turning point ... and it's certainly a historic event for American Jews."

A Torah in Space

Astronaut Dr. Jeffery Hoffman (b.1944) has been in space several times to fix the Hubbell telescope. On a mission in 1996, Hoffman carried a Torah on board the space shuttle Columbia. Hoffman, a member of Congregation Or Hadash in Houston, Texas, had long dreamed of taking a Torah into space, but size was a problem. The Torah had to be small enough to fit among his personal gear, yet big enough to be used by his congregation when he returned. Klein Brothers of Brooklyn, New York, produced a Torah that met both specifications.

The Torah measured 7 inches long and 4 inches in diameter. Like all Torah scrolls, it contains the text of the first five books of Moses, and was hand-written by a scribe using a goose quill and vegetable-based ink, as prescribed by Jewish law.

Reflecting on this particular mission, Hoffman wrote for the web site of Congregation Or Hadash (members.aol.com/orhadash1/sptorah.htm), "Astronauts are human beings, and when we travel we take with us our culture and heritage. It is important to me to take my Jewish heritage with me, as well."

As part of the world's largest collection of Space Judaica, the Torah is kept at Congregation Or Hadash in the Wolfe Center of Seven Acres Jewish Geriatric Center. The Space Judaica collection represents the synagogue's commitment to creating a dynamic synagogue community to embrace the future.

Rabbi Sally Priesand (b.1946)

Sally Priesand is the first American woman to be ordained as a rabbi. In 1963, when she was seeking admission to the rabbinical program at Hebrew Union College, the Reform movement's theological seminary, Priesand received a letter of rejection that said, "We would have to inform you candidly that we do not know what opportunities are available for women in the active rabbinate, since we have, as yet, not ordained any women. Most women prefer to enter the field of Jewish religious education."

But even centuries of Jewish tradition could not resist the feminist movement. As the 1960s came to an end, women already studying at Hebrew Union College and at the Jewish Theological Seminary began to see changes in thinking that suggested the exclusion of women from the rabbinate might finally be coming to an end. Priesand was admitted to the rabbinical program at Hebrew Union College in 1968 and was ordained on June 3, 1972.

Her first job was at New York's Stephen Wise Free Synagogue, where she served as assistant rabbi. In 1981 she became the senior rabbi at the Monmouth Reform Temple in Tinton Falls, New Jersey. Priesand paved the way for many other women to enter the rabbinate.

Dr. Judith Resnik (1949–1986)

In 1984, Dr. Judith Resnik became the second American woman to travel in space, serving as mission specialist on the first voyage of the space shuttle Discovery.

Born in Akron, Ohio, Resnik earned her B.S. degree in Electrical Engineering from Carnegie Mellon University in Pittsburgh and her doctorate in Electrical Engineering from the University of Maryland. She was selected as an astronaut in 1978. After completing a one-year training program with NASA, she was assigned to work on a variety of projects in support of the space shuttle's development, including experimental software, the remote manipulator system, and astronaut training techniques.

On January 28, 1986, as millions of people watched, Resnik boarded the Challenger space shuttle for her second flight into space. The shuttle was launched from the Kennedy Space Center in Florida at 11:38 a.m. Resnik, along with the other crew members, died when the Challenger exploded just seconds after launch.

The right stuff
In total, Dr. Judith Resnick logged more than 144 hours in space as a mission specialist aboard the space shuttle Discovery. While in orbit, Resnik's responsibility was to photograph Discovery's robotic arm to inspect a piece of ice that had formed on the side of the shuttle. Because of her work, the crew was able to knock off the ice.

7

Judaism in America: Today and Tomorrow

ON THE DAYS JUST BEFORE SEPTEMBER 11, 2001, MOST JEWS WERE busy preparing for Rosh HaShanah and, in typical fashion, many commented that the holidays were coming "early." Synagogues across the United States were getting ready for the big crowds who always come during the important holidays of Rosh HaShanah and Yom Kippur. And then came September 11.

On that day, the United States experienced the worst terrorist attack in its history. Four commercial jets were hijacked. The hijackers crashed two into the World Trade Center in New York City and one into the Pentagon outside Washington, D.C. The fourth plane crashed in Pennsylvania after passengers tried to retake control. In all, more than 3,000 people were killed.

In Greenwich, Connecticut, that day, after the terrible tragedies in New York, Washington, D.C., and Pennsylvania, a meeting of the Fellowship of Clergy was convened by its president, Rabbi Mitchell Hurvitz. Within a very short time, its members had planned an interfaith prayer service and vigil to be held that night at the synagogue. More than 1,000 people attended. Similar prayer services were held in churches and synagogues across the country, and the message was clear: People needed the comfort of others, and people needed God.

Memorial services were scheduled somewhere almost every day. At one service held at Yankee Stadium in New York, clergy of all faiths prayed for

The Jewish Calendar

The Jewish calendar follows the cycles of the moon (unlike the calendar in common use, which follows the cycles of the sun). Each month begins with the new moon. Each new day begins at sunset. That is because when the book of Genesis in the Bible describes how God created the world, it says, "and there was evening and there was morning, one day."

There are 12 months in the Jewish calendar, alternating between 29 and 30 days long. But since Jewish holidays are meant to be celebrated in specific seasons—and since having just 12 short months a year would soon move the spring holidays into summer and the summer holidays into fall—an extra leap month is added seven out of every 19 years.

The Jewish year begins in the fall with Rosh HaShanah. The months are: Tishri, Heshvan, Kislev, Tevet, Shevat, Adar (Adar II in a leap year), Nisan, Iyar, Sivan, Tammuz, Av, and Elul.

According to tradition, Jews count the years from the day of Creation. This date was determined by adding up the number of years lived by men in various generations as described in the Bible and by certain traditions. For example, it is generally agreed that there were 400 years between the birth of Isaac and the exodus from Egypt. In September 2002, Jews celebrated Rosh HaShanah by ushering in the year 5763.

PRECEDING PAGE
In memory
Cantor Ken Cohen of Temple Sholom in Greenwich, Connecticut, sings in Hebrew during an interfaith memorial service for the victims of the September 11 terrorist attack.

comfort. Rabbis, priests, ministers, and imams all brought one message: As human beings we are, indeed, responsible for one another. New York City's Mayor Rudy Giuliani and New York Governor George Pataki called on citizens to band together, and President George W. Bush asked all Americans to reach out to their neighbors, to help and support them.

A December 17, 2002, article in *The New York Times* ("A New, Inclusive Era of the Holiday party") noted, "The many gods in American life are alive and well at the White House, where never before have so many religions converged in such a powerful surge of faith and politics." In 2001, in addition to the national celebration of Christmas, President Bush hosted a Chanukkah party featuring kosher food and celebrated the Muslim holiday of Eid al-Fitr, marking the end of the Muslim holy month of Ramadan. Newspapers and magazines featured numerous articles that described how Americans were turning back to their religious traditions to find solace.

The Challenges of Pluralism and Secularism

A few years ago, as Americans faced the new millennium, religious leaders of all faiths began to look at the state of religion. Jewish leaders remarked that perhaps, at the turn of the 21st century, it was, in the words of Charles Dickens, "the best of times and the worst of times." While Jewish Americans lead fulfilling lives in a society that values pluralism and democracy, there seemed to be deep divisions among the major denominations. It seemed that Jews could no longer speak among themselves and that attempts at dialogue were futile.

On the other hand, leaders representing the Orthodox, Conservative, Reform, and Reconstructionist movements could agree on one thing: The future of American Jews would be in their own hands; Jews would be free to choose a path for themselves.

These leaders also agreed on one very serious problem facing American Jews: intermarriage. Just as each wave of Jewish immigrants developed their own distinctive patterns of Jewish life, second- and third-generation Jewish Americans successfully assimilated into American society. But assimilation, along with elimination of quotas that once excluded Jewish students from many college campuses, has led to intermingling among a variety of cultures.

At the turn of the 20th century, there was little or no social contact between Jews and non-Jews. At the turn of the 21st century, statistics indicate that nearly 50 percent of Jews are marrying out of their faith. In December, many more families are facing the "December dilemma"—Mom is in church, Dad is in synagogue; Mom decorates the Christmas tree and Dad lights the Chanukkah candles. According to a December 15, 1997, article in *Newsweek* magazine ("A Matter of Faith" by Jerry Adler), "We have always been a nation of seekers, and now no one is bound by the religious fault lines of the past."

Both the Reform and Conservative movements have made significant investments in creating outreach programs to bring intermarried couples into their synagogues. The Reform movement's decision to consider a child Jewish if his or her father is Jewish is a big departure from traditional Jewish law, which traces religious descent through the mother. This change has made it possible for children whose fathers are Jewish to participate in religious education classes and other programs offered by the synagogue. In addition, most Reform congregations have a policy that encourages intermarried families to enjoy the full privileges of membership in the congregation.

The Conservative movement has also created an array of opportunities for non-Jewish partners. However, non-Jewish spouses are not considered as full members of the congregation. The Conservative movement considers children born to Jewish mothers as being Jewish and does not accept the Reform decision regarding Jewish fathers.

Jewish Community Centers across North America welcome all Jews and intermarried families, providing them with a friendly, non-threatening gateway into the Jewish community.

The Challenge of Feminism

There can be no doubt that the mixing of feminism with Judaism has made significant changes in the Jewish community. In the 1940s and 1950s, an Orthodox family would never have considered a *bat mitzvah* celebration for their daughter; only the Reform and Conservative movements included this celebration as a daughter's rite of passage into Jewish maturity. Now, however, Orthodox families would not think about the possibility of *not* celebrating a daughter's *bat mitzvah*.

Today there are hundreds of female rabbis serving congregations, community centers, schools, and non-profit agencies, and their im-

Pioneering rabbi
Rabbi Sally Priesand, the first American woman to be a rabbi, was ordained in 1972. The Reform movement now has many female rabbis. Rabbi Amy Eilberg was the first Conservative Jewish woman ordained at Jewish Theological Seminary, in 1985. The Orthodox movement still does not ordain women as rabbis.

Jewish Feminist Leaders

In 1963, writer Betty Friedan (born Bettye Naomi Goldstein in 1921 in Peoria, Illinois) published *The Feminine Mystique*, a book that changed the way many women think about themselves. According to Friedan, "We can no longer ignore that voice within women that says: I want something more than my husband and my children and my home." The book sold more than 2 million copies, and catapulted Friedan into the position of spokeswoman for the American feminist movement. In 1966, she established the National Organization for Women (NOW), which quickly became the principal feminist advocacy group in the United States. The majority of women who took on leadership positions in NOW were Jewish. Friedan's commitment to women's equality "was really a passion against injustice," she says, "which originated from my feelings of the injustice of anti-Semitism."

Gloria Steinem (b.1934), the founder and editor of *Ms.* magazine, is the granddaughter of Pauline Perlmutter Steinem, who served as president of the Ohio Women's Suffrage Association.

At about the same time, there were other Jewish women who were leaders in industry, business, arts, and politics: Helene Rubinstein and Estée Lauder in the cosmetics industry; Diane von Furstenberg and Hellen Galladin in the clothing industry; Sherry Landsing and Barbara Walters in movies and television; Bella Abzug, Madeline Kunin, and Elizabeth Holtzman in politics. These women helped break down the barriers that held back talented, able women from achieving all they are capable of.

pact is powerful. Female rabbis have empowered a generation of young women to seek out opportunities to serve their communities as professionals. Much of the creative energy in contemporary Judaism is due to its female rabbis and lay leaders.

Other professional Jewish women serve their communities in a multitude of positions, including congregation presidents, day school and supplementary congregational religious school directors, and executive directors of federations, community centers, and synagogues.

Both the Reform and the Conservative movements accept women into their respective seminaries and ordain them as rabbis. While the Orthodox movement does not accept women to study at their seminaries or to become rabbis, a growing number of Orthodox women have completed advanced studies in Jewish law. This makes them eligible to become "spiritual counselors" in a small number of New York Orthodox congregations.

Worldwide Challenges

Another challenge confronting Jewish Americans is the nature of their responsibility toward Jews living in Israel and in other countries around the world. Jews are currently facing a variety of troubling and challenging situations. After a century of repression by Communist governments, there is a Jewish reawakening in Russia and Poland. However, these Jews often lack the most basic religious education, and need help rediscovering their identity. And, due to financial collapse, the Jews of Argentina are facing many hardships. American Jews have begun to reorganize federated agencies to address these and other new realities at home and around the world.

Zionism has a new set of objectives to achieve now that Israel has been in existence for more than 50 years. Reform and Conservative Jews who live in Israel face new questions about the right to practice Judaism independent of a powerful, politically based Orthodox party that refuses to recognize the legitimacy of liberal Jewish lifestyles.

Will there be opportunities for the Reform and Conservative movements to grow and address a liberal Judaism for Israelis? Who will provide funding for them? Will there ever be peace between Israel and its Arab neighbors? When will the cycle of violence end? What will be the nature of the relationship between American Jews and Israelis? These questions and others like them need to be addressed.

However, one thing is clear: Jewish Americans will continue to debate about Israeli politics and they will, for the most part, continue to defend Israel and celebrate her achievements.

Possibilities for the Future

Not too long ago, *Moment Magazine*, a magazine for Jewish culture and opinion, conducted a symposium, posing many of the same questions posed in this chapter to a group of Jewish leaders. Their answers, reported in the December 1977 issue of *Moment,* were mixed.

Alan Dershowitz, a Harvard Law School professor, said in his article, "Rampant Assimilation," "Jewish ideas will become more assimilated into the mainstream. Our future depends not upon how we look, but rather on what we do."

In Dershowitz' opinion, Jews are beginning a new course. Jewish people are no longer persecuted or forced into living in ghettos, and there are significantly fewer demonstrations of anti-Semitism than in the past. Now is the time, according to Dershowitz, for Jews to "write new literature, create new philosophies, sing new songs, and paint new pictures reflective of this new outlook."

Julius Lester, an African American and a professor of Jewish Studies at the University of Massachusetts in Amherst, suggested in his article, "Reconservadoxy," that in the 21st century Jews will describe themselves as "Reconservadox." He means that Jews will select elements of the major American Jewish movements and combine them all together in ways that suit their needs.

Still others suggest that American Jews will not identify themselves as belonging to any denomination. Because of intermarriage, assimilation, and adoption, Jews will no longer be an ethnically distinctive group.

However, evidence suggests that the Jewish community has a strong desire to provide social and religious programs in a diverse and pluralistic environment. Lay leaders, together with religious leaders of all the Jewish movements, are working to find ways to enable Jews to connect in a shared commitment to study the Jewish texts and devote themselves to living according to Jewish tradition.

Synagogues, Jewish Community Centers, summer camps, and youth groups across denominational lines are working together to create opportunities for Jews to meet, and to empower individuals to seek connections between Jewish texts, ideas, and practices.

Jews remain a minority in the United States. However, like all other Americans, they face the challenges of dealing with an aging population that will require facilities to meet their needs. Community leaders will have to address the changing nature of Jewish identity as one generation grows old and another grows up, and the means by which Jews express their identity in America.

Other challenges will include providing services for single-parent families and acknowledging alternate lifestyles, providing food, shelter and clothing for the poor, educating the younger generation, and addressing issues related to substance abuse.

The Jewish leadership recognizes the need to provide a wide array of opportunities for Jews to connect with one another. They understand that some Jews may choose to relate to Judaism as individuals rather than as part of a congregation. For these individuals, a solitary spiritual encounter may take place via the Internet. Still others will embrace alternate ways of seeking spiritual experiences—retreats, workshops, and a variety of classes will be created for those seeking to forge an intimate connection with God.

OUR COMMON DESTINY
Rabbi Irving Greenberg, president of the Jewish Life Network, a think tank advocating Jewish education and pluralism, wrote in a March 1998 article for *Hadassah Magazine* ("A House Dividing"), "Pluralism is the most important ingredient in Jewish unity." He calls on all Jewish groups, including Jews who are not affiliated with any denomination or movement, to reconnect. "We must now use our freedom to reaffirm mutual community and common destiny."

GLOSSARY

anti-Semitism hostility toward or discrimination against all Jews

ashkenazim Jews who come from northern and eastern Europe

atonement the reconciliation of God and humanity

B.C.E. these letters stand for the phrase "Before the Common Era," and are used in the same way as historians use the letters B.C.—which stand for "Before Christ"—to refer to events that happened before the year 1 in the common calendar.

bar (or bat) mitzvah when one becomes an adult under Jewish law (13 for a boy, 12 for a girl)

bond a certificate issued by a government or a public company, promising to repay borrowed money within a specific time at a fixed rate of interest

borscht belt a group of hotels in the Catskill Mountains built as summer resorts mainly for Jewish clients

burlesque comic entertainment that was popular in America from the 1870s; it consisted of songs and dances performed by women and comedy routines performed by men, often using vulgar vocabulary with sexually suggestive language

C.E. these letters stand for the phrase "Common Era," and are used in the same way as historians use the letters A.D.—an abbreviation for the Latin term Anno Domini— to refer to events that happened after the birth of Christ

cantor a person who leads the prayers of the congregation in a synagogue

circumcision removal of the foreskin of the penis

cobbler a person who repairs shoes

concentration camp a prison camp used to detain political prisoners; the phrase has come to be associated with Nazi Germany, where concentration camps were used for slave labor and mass murder

converso a Spanish Jew in the 14th and 15th centuries who pretended to convert to Christianity in order to avoid the punishments of the Inquisition, but who secretly remained Jewish

diaspora the dispersal of Jewish people throughout the world after the destruction of the Temple in Jerusalem in 70 C.E.

exodus a mass departure of people; the book of Exodus in the Bible recounts the Jewish people's departure from Egypt

flatboat a boat with a flat bottom, used for transportation in shallow water

genesis the origin or beginning of something; the book of Genesis in the Bible recounts the creation of the world and the beginnings of the Jewish people

genocide the deliberate extermination of a people or a nation

ghetto a part of a city occupied by a minority group; the word was first applied to the Jewish quarter in Venice, where Jews were forced, by law, to live in a segregated area

greenhorn an inexperienced newcomer

halakhah the body of Jewish law

Hasidim members of a Jewish mystical sect that emphasizes the joy and spiritual nature of a relationship with God

Holocaust the mass murder of Jews by Nazis during World War II

intermarriage marriage between people of different religions, races, or backgrounds

Kabbalah   the tradition of Jewish mystical thought

kosher   following the Jewish dietary laws

Kristallnacht   November 9, 1938, literally, "Night of Broken Glass"; this vandalism and violence against Jews in Germany is often referred to as the official beginning of the Holocaust

liturgy   the preset forms and prayers for public worship

matzah   unleavened bread eaten during Passover

melodrama   a dramatic piece that appeals broadly to the emotions

menorah   a special candleholder with eight branches that is lit on Chanukkah

monotheism   a belief in one God

omnipotent   all-powerful

omniscient   able to see all

pharaoh   the king or emperor of ancient Egypt; pharaohs were considered to be gods

piecework   when workers are paid a set rate per unit they produce

pilgrimage   a long journey or expedition undertaken for a holy purpose

pluralism   a form of society in which the minority members maintain their independent beliefs or traditions

pogrom   an organized and officially sanctioned massacre, originally of Jews in Russia

profane   not part of what is sacred or Biblical

psalm   a sacred song or hymn

quartermaster   an army officer in charge of securing living arrangements (quarters) and rations for the soldiers

rabbi   a person appointed as a Jewish religious leader

reader's desk   the special platform in a synagogue where people read the Torah

refusnik   a Jew living in the Soviet Union who applied for, and was denied, permission to emigrate

Sabbath   a day of rest and religious observance; Saturday is the Jewish Sabbath day

secular   not religious

seder   a special religious service held on Passover

sephardim   from the Hebrew word meaning "Spain," sephardim are Jews who lived on the Iberian Peninsula and along the Mediterranean Sea

settlement house   a community center where new immigrants could learn English and American culture

shirtwaist   a woman's blouse that resembles a man's shirt

sweatshop   a factory where workers are subject to long hours, low wages and unhealthy conditions

synagogue   a Jewish house of worship

Talmud   a collection of interpretations of the laws found in the Torah

Tanakh   the Hebrew Bible

telegraph   a way of sending messages over long distances by using an electrical signal

tenement   a building made of many small apartments that does not offer much in the way of sanitation, safety, or comfort

theology   a system of religious thinking; the beliefs of a religion

Torah   the first five books of the Bible (Genesis, Exodus, Leviticus, Numbers, and Deuteronomy), containing the laws of God

vaudeville   a program that contains a variety of acts, including musical performances, magicians, dancing, jugglers, and comic routines

yeshiva   any Jewish school; a school for training rabbis

Yiddish   a language used by Eastern European Jews, made of words from the German, Polish, and Russian languages and written in Hebrew letters

Zionism   an international movement calling for the establishment of a Jewish state in Palestine

Time Line

1654	A shipload of Jews arrives in New Amsterdam from Recife, Brazil.
1680	A Jewish community is formed in Newport, Rhode Island.
1733	A Jewish community is formed in Savannah, Georgia.
1750	A Jewish community is formed in Charleston, South Carolina.
1729	The first synagogue in North America is established in New York City.
1824–33	The American Reform movement begins with its first synagogue in Charleston, South Carolina.
1834	The mass immigration of Jews from Germanic lands begins.
1843	The first Jewish fraternal organization, B'nai Brith, is established in New York.
1887	The Jewish Theological Seminary of America, a rabbinical school for the Conservative movement, opens in New York.
1897	*The Jewish Daily Forward*, a socialist newspaper written in Yiddish, begins publication in New York.
1912	Henrietta Szold establishes Hadassah, the largest women's Zionist organization in the world.
1915	Yeshiva University, the first Orthodox institute of higher education, opens in New York.
1935	The American Jewish Congress declares a boycott on Germany to protest the deportation of Jews to ghettos and, later, concentration camps.
1943	500 Orthodox rabbis participate in a march to the White House, where they request a meeting with President Franklin D. Roosevelt to discuss an American response to the Holocaust. Roosevelt will not meet with them.
1948	The state of Israel is established. President Harry Truman becomes the first world leader to recognize the new state.
1967	American Jewish volunteers go to Israel to help with the war effort. Huge financial contributions pour in from American Jews to help Israel.
1973	Henry Kissinger becomes secretary of state of the United States, the highest post ever held by a Jew, and Abraham Beame is elected the first Jewish mayor of New York.
2000	Senator Joseph Lieberman of Connecticut is picked by presidential candidate Al Gore to run for vice president of the United States.

RESOURCES

Reading List

Altman, Linda Jacobs, *The Creation of Israel*. San Diego, Calif.: Lucent Books, 1998.

Bierman, Carol and Laurie McGaw, *Journey to Ellis Island*. New York: Hyperion Press, 1998.

Brody, Seymour, *Jewish Heroes and Heroines of America: 150 True Stories of American Jewish Heroism*. Hollywood, Calif.: Lifetime Books, 1996.

Chaikin, Miriam, *Menorahs, Mezuzas, and Other Jewish Symbols*. Boston: Clarion Books, 1990.

David, Rabbi Jo and Daniel B. Syme, *The Book of the Jewish Life*. New York: Union of American Hebrew Congregations, 1998.

Finkelstein, Norman H., *Heeding the Call : Jewish Voices in America's Civil Rights Struggle*. Philadelphia: Jewish Publication Society, 1997.

Holliday, Laurel, ed., *Children in the Holocaust and World War II: Their Secret Diaries*. New York: Pocket Books, 1995.

Morrison, Martha A. and Stephen F. Brown. *Judaism (World Religions Series)* rev. ed. New York: Facts On File, 2002.

Muggamin, Howard, *The Jewish Americans*. Broomall, Penn.: Chelsea House Publishers, 1995.

Stanley, Jerry, *Frontier Merchants: How Lionel & Barron Jacobs and the Jewish Pioneers Settled the West*. New York: Crown Publications, 1998.

Wylen, Stephen M., *The Book of the Jewish Year*. New York: Union of American Hebrew Congregations, 1998.

Resources on the Web

American Jewish Historical Society
www.ajhs.org
Virtual tours of the Society's exhibitions, research resources, and a special section on Jews in sports.

The Holocaust History Project
www.holocaust-history.org
An archive of documents, photographs, recordings, and essays regarding the Holocaust.

Jewish-American History on the Web
www.jewish-history.com
Details of the roles Jews played in every era of American history, plus a database that enables you to look up Jewish ancestors in America.

The Jewish Calendar
www.ou.org/chagim/default.htm
All the holidays in the Jewish calendar, what they mean, and when they are celebrated.

Mish Mash—Linking Judaism Worldwide
www.mish-mash.ca
A vast site of links to thousands of other Jewish sites, plus Ask-a-Rabbi and a section just for kids.

The Museum of American Jewish History
www.nmajh.org
A virtual tour of the Museum of American Jewish History in Philadelphia, and a Jewish history timeline.

Museum of Jewish Heritage
www.mjhnyc.org
A virtual tour of the Museum of Jewish Heritage in New York.

United States Holocaust Memorial Museum
www.ushmm.org
A virtual tour of the United States Holocaust Memorial Museum in Washington, D.C., plus educational and research resources.

INDEX

Note: *Italic* page numbers refer to illustrations.

Deuteronomy, 10, 73
diaspora, 11
Dreyfus, Alfred, 93
Dubinsky, David, 83, 98–99
Dutch West India Company, 23, 24–25

Eastern Europe
    immigration from, 39, 41–42, 49, 53, 77–80, 81, 105
    during World War II, 53
education
    importance of, 65, 68–69
    for lay leaders, 49
    in pioneer times, 38
    rabbinical training, 45, 48, 50, 102
    religious discrimination in, 69–70, 92
    Russia in the 1800s, 37
    yeshivas, 50, 107
Egypt, ancient, 8, 9, 17, 27
Einhorn, Rabbi David, 33–34
Einstein, Albert, 70
Eisner, Michael, 109
Elhanan, Rabbi Isaac, 50
Ellis Island, 40, 65
ethical codes, 12, 19, 27, 44
exile
    from Brazil in the 1600s, 24
    from Jerusalem, 10, 11
    land and nationhood, 13–14
    a portable nation, 11
    from Spain in the 1400s, 11, 20–21, 22–23
Exodus (in the Torah), 8, 9, 10
Exodus (ship), 96

family issues, 16, 87, 115–116, 119
Federated Jewish Charities, 79
federated system of charity, 79–80, 84, 85–87, 95
Female Hebrew Benevolent Society, 76
feminist movement, 110, 116–117
Ferber, Edna, 65
festival days, 16–18
Fettman, Dr. Martin, 71
Five Books of Moses, See Torah
foods with Jewish roots, 64, 87
Frank, Leo, 92, 93
Frankel, Rabbi Jacob, 35
Frankel, Rabbi Zechariah, 45–46
Friedan, Betty, 117

Galveston Plan, 80, 102
Gatling, Richard, 91
Geffen, Peter, 97
Gemara, 47

gemilut chasadim, 27, 73–74, 75–76
Genesis, 7, 10, 13, 114
Germany
    immigrants from, 37–39, 41–42, 54
    Nazism during World War II, 18, 52–55
Gershwin, George, 59–60
ghettos, 32, 41, 53
Glickman, Marty, 68
global challenges, 117–118
God, role in Judaism, 9, 9, 12, 19, 44
Goldberg, Arthur, 94
Goldberger, Joseph, 70
Golden, Harry, 69
Goldfaden, Abraham, 58
Goldwater, Barry, 38
Goldwater, Michael, 38
Goldwyn, Samuel, 62, 105–106, 106
Gompers, Samuel, 83
Goodman, Andrew, 98
Goodman, Benny, 63
Gore, Al, 89, 108, 109
Gottlieb, Eddie, 67
Gould, Jay, 89
Graham, Charles, 90
Grant, Gen. Ulysses S., 35
Gratz, Barnard and Michael, 28–29, 31
Great Depression, 83, 85
Green, Shawn, 67, 68
Greenberg, Hank, 67, 68
Greenberg, Rabbi Irving, 119
Greenspan, Alan, 108
Grove, Andrew, 71
Gruber, Ruth, 55
Gruening, Ernest, 66
Guggenheim, Meyer, 90, 91
Guggenheim, Peggy, 65
Guggenheim family, 39, 65, 90–91

Hadassah, 94, 95
Hadassah Magazine, 119
halakhah, 12–13, 43–44, 47
Harding, Pres. Warren, 91
Hasidim and Hasidism, 50–52, 51, 99
de Hass, Jacob, 103
Hebrew, 27, 43, 45, 48, 66
Hebrew Bible. See Tanakh
Hebrew Immigrant Aid Society (HIAS), 43
Hebrews, The, 67
Hebrew Union College, 45, 102, 110
Herzl, Theodor, 93, 103
Heschel, Rabbi Abraham Joshua, 98, 98
Hillquit, Morris, 81–82

Hirsch, Rabbi Emil, 97
historical background
    ancient Israelites, 7–9
    colonial times, 21, 24–31
    immigrants. See exile; immigration
    laws and leaders, 9–11
    pioneer times, 31–32, 37–39
    revolutionary times, 21, 22, 29, 31, 32
    World War II. See Holocaust
Hitler, Adolph, 52–53, 54, 86
Hoffman, Dr. Jeffery, 110
holidays and feast days, 16–19
Holocaust
    day of remembrance, 18–19
    and the hasidim, 51
    overview, 52–55
    social welfare for survivors, 86, 95
    and Zionism, 94–95
Holocaust Memorial Museum, 53
Holtzman, Ken, 68
Hoover, Pres. Herbert, 91
Horowitz, Scott, 71
Hughes, Sarah, 67
human rights, 80–83, 117–118
Hyneman, Elias Leon, 34–35

immigration. See also exile
    aid society, 43
    to Central U.S., the Galveston Plan, 79, 80, 102
    colonial times, 21, 24–31
    from Eastern Europe, 39, 41–42, 49, 53, 77–80, 81, 105
    from Germany, 37–39, 41–42, 77, 83, 91
    photography collection, 65
    pioneer times, 31–32, 37–39, 76–77
    revolutionary times, 21, 22, 29, 31, 32
    role of European home town, 79
    from Russia, 81
    U.S. laws, 53, 102
    to U.S. in the 1600s, 23–24, 27–31
Industrial Removal Office, 79, 80
Intel Corporation, 71
intermarriage, 115–116, 119
International Ladies Garment Workers Union, 83, 98
Internet. See web sites
Isaac, 7, 15, 114
Isaacs, Rabbi Samuel, 35
Isaiah, 74
Islam, 13, 114